The Poems of Queen Elizabeth I

BROWN UNIVERSITY
BICENTENNIAL PUBLICATIONS

Studies in the Fields of General Scholarship

THE POEMS OF
Queen Elizabeth I

EDITED BY LEICESTER BRADNER

BROWN UNIVERSITY PRESS

PROVIDENCE, RHODE ISLAND

Designed by David Ford
Type set in 10 point Linotype Janson by Crimson Printing Company
Printed by Crimson Printing Company on University Text
Bound by Stanhope Bindery

ACKNOWLEDGMENTS

IN COLLECTING these poems and in preparing the text I have been greatly aided by Professor William A. Ringler of the University of Chicago and Dr. Richard W. Hunt of the Bodleian Library in Oxford. Most of the excellencies, and none of the defects, of this edition are the result of their interest and help. My lifelong colleague at Brown, the late Charles Arthur Lynch, spent many hours, now cherished because never to be repeated, going over the translations from Latin and Greek with me. The staffs of the Brown and Harvard Libraries and of the Bodleian Library have been most helpful at all times in making my work easier.

I wish to thank Mr. Eric W. White of the Poetry Book Society in London for calling my attention to the poem written in Queen Elizabeth's psalter and for permission to base my text on that given in the Society's *Bulletin* for November 1958. I am also grateful to the Ohio State University Press for permission to base my text of "The Triumph of Petrarch" on Miss Hughey's in her edition of the Arundel Harington manuscript. To Mr. A. R. A. Hobson of Sotheby's I am indebted for information about a manuscript containing poems attributed to Queen Elizabeth.

Finally, I am most grateful to Professor James E. Phillips of the University of California at Los Angeles, whose discovery of a new poem attributed to the Queen I learned of at the last minute, for sending me proof-sheets of his article and for permission to use his translation of this Latin poem. *Renaissance News* has also kindly permitted me to use this copyrighted material.

LEICESTER BRADNER

Brown University
January 16, 1964

CONTENTS

INTRODUCTION

THE ONLY attempt previously made to collect Queen Elizabeth's writings in verse was an article published by Ewald Flügel in *Anglia* in 1892. Flügel had seen many, though not all, of the manuscripts and gives a careful transcription of the texts. He was not aware of the existence of the verse translations from Boethius, Horace, and Plutarch in the Public Record Office, which were published by Miss Caroline Pemberton seven years later in the Early English Text Society series, nor did he know of the translation from Petrarch in the Arundel Harington manuscript, which was first made public by Miss Ruth Hughey in 1960. Furthermore, Flügel made no attempt to investigate the relative authenticity of the pieces he published. I have thought it worth while, therefore, to perform this task and to make available a volume in which all of the Queen's genuine, dubious, and even definitely spurious poems are brought together in one place along with all the relevant evidence concerning them. Although no one would claim that she deserved the name of a real poet, her writings form part of the great body of English literature. No excuses are needed for attempting to throw more light on anything, however minor, connected with that most extraordinary woman.

Horace Walpole, in his *Royal and Noble Authors* published in 1758, undertook to make a list of all of Elizabeth's writings, and his work was enlarged by Thomas Park, who brought out a new edition of the book in 1806. Even though Walpole's uncritical acceptance of seventeenth-century attributions foisted upon the Queen a number of rebuses and other ephemeral quips which she probably never wrote, his pioneer work has been of great use to scholars ever since. But aside from this cataloguing activity almost nothing has been done in the way of scholarly work on this material. Miss Pemberton's notes throw some light on Elizabeth's methods of translation; but, as G. B. Riddlehough pointed out in an article in the *Journal of English and Germanic Philology* (XLV, 88–94) in 1946, her ignorance of the different readings found in Renaissance texts of the classics often made her comments unreliable. A thorough study of Elizabeth's work as a translator is much to be desired. Whatever contributions are made to such a study here should be considered mere preliminaries.

The Queen's literary work may be divided into three groups: prose, original poems, and translations. Of her prose we need not speak here, except to remark that she had a genuine gift for that sort of vigorous eloquence which is so well illustrated by her famous Tilbury speech to her army and by the almost equally famous "golden speech" to her last parliament. She also had a ready wit in adapting her words to the situation at hand, a quality which contributed no little to her popularity in her many public appearances.

The great problem of the original poems is that of determining authorship. A group of sixteen poems, some in manuscript, some in print, and some in both, have come down to us. None of them is in the Queen's own handwriting. In some cases, such as that of "The Doubt of Future Foes," the evidence of manuscript attribution and provenance is eminently satisfactory; but in others, notably "When I Was Fair and

Young," considerable doubt exists. One is thrown back on intangibles like style and thought, where critics may disagree. In at least one case the unanimous attributions of the manuscripts are in conflict with my own opinion of what Elizabeth would or would not have written. This is "On Monsieur's Departure," supposed by some to be about Anjou and by others to be about Essex. Unless this poem was intentionally written for political effect I cannot believe that the Queen would ever have committed to writing personal feelings of this kind, particularly as they show her in a light which would not have pleased her. Someone else, however, might have written the poem and circulated it, either as an expression of the Queen's probable feelings or for some kind of political propaganda. Nevertheless, in view of the complete agreement of the manuscript attribution, I have felt obliged to include it among the genuine poems.

The poems which are surely hers are very characteristic. They show her courage, her scorn of fortune, her belief in herself, and her hatred of sedition. They are written in the rough-hewn, vigorous moralistic style of the middle of the sixteenth century, the style of Richard Edwards, Nicholas Grimald, and Jasper Heywood. She uses octosyllabics and poulter's couplets rather than pentameter most of the time. Undoubtedly the best of them is her defiance of Mary's plots against her in "The Doubt of Future Foes." Its imagery is almost entirely drawn from the elementary forces of nature: the ebb and flow of tides, the clouds and the winds and the rain, sowing and reaping of crops, and sailing ships seeking harbor. Even the sword of retributive justice in the last couplet cuts off not human heads but the tops of trees which have grown too high. Though doubts exile her present joy, her wit (i.e. intelligence) has warned her to deal with the situation, and there is not a word of fear in the poem.

The original poems deal with actual situations in Elizabeth's life. The translations, on the other hand, reflect her humanistic education and the reading thought suitable for forming the minds of princes. Many of the themes—praise of virtue, defiance of fortune, attack on slander and suspicion—remind us of her original poems. Out of what must have been a fairly wide reading in the more serious side of classical literature under Ascham's direction she chose to translate those things which were most central to her own thought. The circumstances under which they were done were varied and sometimes obscure to us, and the dates range from her childhood version of the Thirteenth Psalm to the translations of Plutarch and Horace made when she was sixty-five.

Her version of the Thirteenth Psalm was the only one of these translations to be published in her lifetime. It was printed in 1548 as an end piece to her translation of Margaret of Navarre's *Godly Meditation of the Soul.* The translation of part of Petrarch's *Triumph of Eternity,* which is the most carefully done and most readable of the lot, was probably an exercise for one of her tutors, but we cannot date it exactly. The chorus from Seneca's *Hercules Oetaeus* cannot be dated at all, and possibly is not hers. The special problems involved in it are discussed in the notes. This leaves us with the very interesting material found in the Public Record Office manuscript. Domestic Elizabeth 289 consists of a number of pieces which have been preserved together, all being translations from the classics. In 1593 Elizabeth made a translation of the whole of Boethius' *Consolation of Philosophy* in an incredibly short time and wrote a large part of it in her own hand. Although never revised and corrected, this original copy was preserved, and when in 1598 she translated Plutarch's essay on curiosity from the *Moralia* and part of Horace's *Art of Poetry* these were added to the Boethius and put in the royal archives. A note at the end of the Horace indicates that fair copies were made, but none has been preserved. One can only speculate as to why the Queen snatched time from her many pressing governmental and social duties to dash off these hurried English versions. Her knowledge of Latin and Greek was quite genuine, and there is no evidence that she translated from secondary sources, although it appears that she made use of at least one passage, which is an addition to the Greek, from one of the Latin versions of the *Moralia*. But the extreme literalness of her work is sufficient guarantee that it is the original which she is using. We know that she was proud of her classical learning and enjoyed showing it off. The secretarial computations of time attached to the Boethius certainly suggest that Elizabeth had been boasting of the speed with which she produced it. Since it was a work with which she must have been familiar from youth, she probably never stopped to use a dictionary.

Of the three, the *Consolation of Philosophy* is by far the most interesting and the most poetical. This dialogue is one of the great works of all time, and it was particularly popular during the Renaissance. I think we can hardly doubt that Elizabeth read it during those difficult days under her sister Mary, when fortune was dealing her blows almost as deadly as those suffered by Boethius himself. I suspect that it was a solace to her in many of her troubles and dangers. To translate it into her native tongue in her final days of triumph and security must have been pure pleasure. Unfortunately, her method of doing so all too often does violence to her native tongue. You cannot write good English, sometimes not even intelligible English, by a literal following of Latin word order and construction. One has to puzzle out the meaning of "Eurydicen his Orpheus saw, lost and killed" (Orpheus saw, lost, and killed his Eurydice) and "Whilom she fierce kings cruel destroys" (Whilom she, being cruel, destroys fierce kings). Over her errors in translation I will not pause, for they are mostly attributable to haste rather than to lack of understanding of the Latin. She omits words and whole lines in the Latin, and I am convinced that in a number of places her hand simply did not write down correctly what was in her mind. But possibly the most confusing thing for readers today is her use of the old plural of the verb in *s*. For instance, when she writes "My muses . . . what write I shuld, indites" we must read "My muses indite (i.e. tell me) what I should write." And her spelling is a strange and wonderful world of its own.

Of the metrics of her version of the Boethian metres it is difficult to speak with any confidence. She seems to be striving for a line-by-line translation, and this makes it difficult to know whether she was consciously approximating the Latin verse-lengths in English or whether it merely comes out this way because she takes each word as it comes. At any rate, the result is to give her English verse an interesting variety of form, as far as line length goes. There is no rhyme in any of these translations done in her old age.

In spite of all their faults there is a certain vigor and conciseness about many of Elizabeth's Boethius metres that is all her own. And often, too, there is poetic feeling in spite of the awkward word order. Once one has worked over them and learned to understand her peculiar style and her archaic grammar and spelling one comes to prefer them in many cases to the more facile and readable verse of "I.T." published in 1609 and used by the editor of the Loeb Classical Library volume. And when put against the expanded and diluted prose version of George Colville, published in 1556, they seem almost like the work of a literary genius. A good test case is the opening of the first metre of the first book. Colville renders it as follows:

I that in time of prosperity and flourishing study made pleasant and delectable ditties or verses, alas now being heavy and sad overthrown in adversity, am compelled to feel and taste heaviness and grief. Behold the muses poetical, that is to say the pleasure that is in poets' verses, do appoint me and compel me to write these verses in metre, and the sorrowful verses do wet my wretched face with very watery tears issuing out of my eyes for sorrow.

Here is the Queen's version:

> Rhymes that my growing study once performed,
>   In tears, alas, compelled, woeful staves begin.
> My muses torn, behold, what write I should, indite,
>   Where true woeful verse my face with dole bedews.

And this is I.T.'s:

> I that with youthful heat did verses write
> Must now my woes in doleful tunes indite.
> My work is framed by muses torn and rude,
> And my sad cheeks are with true tears bedewed.

The last specimen is more easily understood by us today, but I am not sure that it is essentially any better. The matter is indeed doleful, but the lines trip along as gaily as if this were Pope writing *The Rape of the Lock.*

Best of all perhaps is her version of the famous lines on the golden age. As in the passage above, I have modernized the spelling so that the reader may not be troubled by extraneous difficulties.

> Happy too much the former age
>   With faithful field content,
> Not lost by sluggish lust,
>   That wonts the long fasts
> To loose by soon-got acorn,
>   That knew not Bacchus' gifts
> With molten honey mixed
>   Nor Serian shining fleece
> With Tyrian venom dyed.
>   Sound sleeps gave the grass,
> Their drink the running stream,
>   Shades gave the highest pine.

The depth they fathomed not,
    Nor wares chosen from far
Made stranger find new shores.
    Then were navies still,
Nor bloodshed by cruel hate
    Had fearful weapons stained.
What first fury to foes should
    Any army raise,
When cruel wounds he saw
    And no reward for blood?
Would God our former [error for *present*] time
    To wonted manners fell,
But greedy getting love burns
    Sorer than Etna with her flames.
O who the first man was
    Of hidden gold the weight
Or gems that willing lurked
    The dear danger digged!

But some may prefer her beautifully simple version of the sixth
metre of Book III, a poem which two centuries earlier had
inspired Chaucer's *Balade of Gentilesse*. Although again I
have modernized the spelling, it is worth while to notice that,
with the exception of *crake* (boast), there is not a single word
in this translation which is not in common use today.

All human kind on earth
    From like beginning comes:
One father is of all,
    One only all doth guide.
He gave to sun the beams
    And horns on moon bestowed;
He men to earth did give
    And signs to heaven.
He closed in limbs our souls
    Fetched from highest seat.
A noble seed therefore brought forth

All mortal folk.
What crake you of your stock
  Or forefathers old?
If your first spring and author
  God you view,
No man bastard be,
  Unless with vice the worst he feed
And leaveth so his birth.

NOTE ON THE TEXT

Except for the translations from Boethius, Horace, and Plutarch none of the material in this book is found in the Queen's own handwriting. Elizabethans spelled as they wished, and copyists were notoriously careless. There is no reason, therefore, to pay any regard to the details of spelling and capitalization in the various manuscripts involved, and I have presented all the poems, with the exceptions noted, in modern spelling. I have not, however, tried to read the Queen's mind and give a reconstructed text. In each case I have faithfully followed the best manuscript or early printed version available and given the variants from other sources in the notes. In a very few cases—notably *rain* instead of *rage* in line 6 of "The Doubt of Future Foes"—I have violated this principle because there seemed to be no doubt at all about the correct reading. But in general I have not departed from the copy text from a merely personal belief that a variant was better. Any reader who prefers a variant may follow the good old Elizabethan custom of taking his pen and emending his own copy.

On the other hand, in dealing with poems written in Elizabeth's hand I have reproduced what she wrote with as much accuracy as I could attain. Even obvious errors I have let stand in the text, though corrections are offered in the notes, in order to show the haste and carelessness with which she wrote. Her writing is often difficult to read and sometimes confusingly scratched out and corrected. Although I have in a number of places corrected Miss Pemberton's readings I have nothing but sympathy for the problems she faced and gratitude for having my own way made easier.

ORIGINAL POEMS

Poems of Undoubted Authorship

WRITTEN WITH A DIAMOND
ON HER WINDOW AT WOODSTOCK

Much suspected by me,
Nothing proved can be,
  Quoth Elizabeth prisoner.

WRITTEN ON A WALL
AT WOODSTOCK

Oh fortune, thy wresting wavering state
Hath fraught with cares my troubled wit,
Whose witness this present prison late
Could bear, where once was joy's loan quit.
Thou causedst the guilty to be loosed   5
From bands where innocents were inclosed,
And caused the guiltless to be reserved,
And freed those that death had well deserved.
But all herein can be nothing wrought,
So God send to my foes all they have thought.   10

WRITTEN IN HER FRENCH PSALTER

No crooked leg, no bleared eye,
　No part deformed out of kind,
Nor yet so ugly half can be
　As is the inward suspicious mind.

THE DOUBT OF FUTURE FOES

The doubt of future foes exiles my present joy,
And wit me warns to shun such snares as threaten mine
　　annoy;
For falsehood now doth flow, and subjects' faith doth
　　ebb,
Which should not be if reason ruled or wisdom weaved
　　the web.
But clouds of joys untried do cloak aspiring minds,　　　5
Which turn to rain of late repent by changed course of
　　winds.
The top of hope supposed the root upreared shall be,
And fruitless all their grafted guile, as shortly ye shall
　　see.
The dazzled eyes with pride, which great ambition
　　blinds,
Shall be unsealed by worthy wights whose foresight
　　falsehood finds.　　　　　　　　　　　　　　　　10
The daughter of debate that discord aye doth sow
Shall reap no gain where former rule still peace hath
　　taught to know.
No foreign banished wight shall anchor in this port;
Our realm brooks not seditious sects, let them elsewhere
　　resort.
My rusty sword through rest shall first his edge employ　15
To poll their tops that seek such change or gape for
　　future joy.

ON FORTUNE

Never think you fortune can bear the sway
Where virtue's force can cause her to obey.

ON MONSIEUR'S DEPARTURE

I grieve and dare not show my discontent,
I love and yet am forced to seem to hate,
I do, yet dare not say I ever meant,
I seem stark mute but inwardly do prate.
  I am and not, I freeze and yet am burned,   5
  Since from myself another self I turned.

My care is like my shadow in the sun,
Follows me flying, flies when I pursue it,
Stands and lies by me, doth what I have done.
His too familiar care doth make me rue it.   10
  No means I find to rid him from my breast,
  Till by the end of things it be supprest.

Some gentler passion slide into my mind,
For I am soft and made of melting snow;
Or be more cruel, love, and so be kind.   15
Let me or float or sink, be high or low.
  Or let me live with some more sweet content,
  Or die and so forget what love ere meant.

Poems of Doubtful Authorship

CHRIST WAS THE WORD

Christ was the Word that spake it;
He took the bread and brake it,
And what the Word did make it,
That I believe and take it.

FOUR KNIGHTS
OF NOTTINGHAMSHIRE

Gervase the gentle, Stanhope the stout,
Markham the lion, and Sutton the lout.

REBUS ON NOEL'S NAME

The word of denial and the letter of fifty
Makes the gentleman's name that will never be thrifty.
    Noel's reply:
The foe to the stomach and the word of disgrace
Shows the gentleman's name with the bold face.

REPLY TO RALEIGH

[Fain would I climb yet fear I to fall.]
If thy heart fail thee, climb not at all.

AN ENGLISH HEXAMETER

Persius a crab-staff, bawdy Martial, Ovid a fine wag.

A LATIN HEXAMETER

Ad Graecas, bone rex, fient mandata Calendas.
[Good king, your orders will be carried out on
the Greek Calends, i.e. never.]

WHEN I WAS FAIR AND YOUNG

When I was fair and young, then favor graced me.
Of many was I sought their mistress for to be,
But I did scorn them all and answered them therefore:
Go, go, go, seek some other where, importune me no
    more.

How many weeping eyes I made to pine in woe,   5
How many sighing hearts I have not skill to show,
But I the prouder grew and still this spake therefore:
Go, go, go, seek some other where, importune me no
    more.

Then spake fair Venus' son, that brave victorious boy,
Saying: You dainty dame, for that you be so coy,   10
I will so pluck your plumes as you shall say no more:
Go, go, go, seek some other where, importune me no
    more.

As soon as he had said, such change grew in my breast
That neither night nor day I could take any rest.
Wherefore I did repent that I had said before: 15
Go, go, go, seek some other where, importune me no
    more.

EPITAPH MADE BY THE
QUEEN'S MAJESTY
AT THE DEATH OF
THE PRINCESS OF ESPINOYE

When the warrior Phoebus goeth to make his round
With a painful course to t'other hemisphere,
A dark shadow, a great horror and a fear
In I know not what clouds environ the ground.
And even so for Pinoy, that fair virtuous lady   5
(Although Jupiter have in this horizon
Made a star of her by the Ariadnian crown),
Mourns, dolor and grief accompany our body.
O Atropos, thou hast done a work perverst,
And as a bird that hath lost both young and nest   10
About the place where it was makes many a turn,
Even so doth Cupid, that infant god of amor,
Fly about the tomb where she lies all in dolor,
Weeping for her eyes wherein he made sojourn.

NOW LEAVE AND LET ME REST

Now leave and let me rest,
Dame Pleasure be content;
Go choose among the best,
My doting days be spent.
By sundry signs I see   5
Thy proffers are but vain,
And wisdom warneth me
That pleasure asketh pain.

And Nature that doth know
How time her steps doth try   10
Gives place to painful woe
And bids me learn to die.
Since all fair earthly things
Soon ripe will soon be rot,

And all that pleasant springs   15
Soon withered, soon forgot.

And youth that yields new joys
That wanton lust desires
In age repents the toys
That reckless youth requires.   20
All which delights I leave
To such as folly trains
By pleasure to deceive
Till they do feel the pains.

And from vain pleasures past   25
I fly and fain would know
The happy life at last
Whereto I hope to go,
For words or wise reports
Or yet examples gone   30
Can bridle youthful sports
Till age comes stealing on.

The pleasant courtly games
That I delighted in,
Mine elder age now shames   35
Such follies to begin,
And all the fancies strange
That fond delight brought forth
I do intend to change
And count them nothing worth.   40

For I by process worn
Am taught to know the skill
What might have been forborne
In my young reckless will.
By which good proof I fleet.   45
From will to wit again
In hope to set my feet
In surety to remain.

REGINAE RESPONSVM

Grata Camena tua est, gratissima dona, Melisse:
    Gratior est animi dulcis imago tui.
At quae tanta movet te causa, quis impetus urget,
    Ex homine ingenuo servus ut esse velis?
Haud nostrum est arctis vates includere septis,   5
    Aut vel tantillum deminuisse caput.
Tu potius liber fieres, laxante patrona
    Vincula, si famula conditione fores.
Sed vatum es princeps; ego vati subdita, dum me
    Materiam celsi carminis ipse legis,   10
Quem regum pudeat tantum coluisse poetam,
    Nos ex semideis qui facit esse deos?

VERSE TRANSLATIONS

THE THIRTEENTH
PSALM OF DAVID

Fools that true faith yet never had
Saith in their hearts, there is no God.
Filthy they are in their practice,
Of them not one is godly wise.
From heaven the Lord on man did look   5
To know what ways he undertook.
All they were vain and went astray,
Not one he found in the right way.
In heart and tongue have they deceit,
Their lips throw forth a poisoned bait.   10
Their minds are mad, their mouths are wode,
And swift they be in shedding blood.
So blind they are, no truth they know,
No fear of God in them will grow.
How can that cruel sort be good,   15
Of God's dear flock which suck the blood?
On him rightly shall they not call,
Despair will so their hearts appall.
At all times God is with the just,
Because they put in him their trust.   20
Who shall therefore from Sion give
That health which hangeth in our belief?
When God shall take from his the smart,
Then will Jacob rejoice in heart.
       Praise to God

PETRARCH'S
TRIUMPH OF ETERNITY
(LINES 1–90)

Amazed to see nought under heaven's cope
Steady and fast, thus to myself I spake:
Advise thee well—on whom doth hang thy hope?
On God, said I, that promise never brake

With those that trust in him. But now I know   5
How erst the fickle world abused me,
Eke what I am and was. And now to go
Or rather fly the nimble time I see,
Blame would I, wist I whom; for all the crime
Is mine that should (not slacking till the last)   10
Have erst unclosed mine eyes before this time.
For truth to say, old wax I all too fast,
But over late God's grace came never yet.
In me also I trust there shall be wrought
Works wonderful and strange by means of it.   15
These said and answer made, thus more I thought:
If none of all these things do stand in stay
That heaven turns and guides, what end at last
Shall follow of their ever turning sway?
While deeper yet my searching mind I cast,   20
A world all new even then it seemed me
In never changing and ever living age,
The sun, the sky with all her stars to see
Dissolved quite with earth and seas that rage,
One made more fair and pleasant in his place.   25
When him that never stayed but erst to change
Each thing was wont wandering in divers race
Stand on one foot I saw; how seemed it strange
All his three parts brought into only one,
And that one fast, so that as wont it was   30
No more so swift it hasted to be gone
But had one show as earth despoiled of grass.
There were not *shall be*, *hath been*, after erst
To irksome, weak and divers state that brought
Our life. As sun doth pierce the glass, so pierced   35
My thought, yea more, for nothing stoppeth thought.
What grace find I to see if I attain
Even face to face the greatest good of all
(No ill which only time gives and again
As first it came with time eke part it shall).   40

The Bull or Fish lodge shall no more the sun,
Whose change doth make a toil now die, now spring,
Now waste, now grow. Oh happy sprights that won
Or shall hereafter stand in the chief ring,
Whose names aye memory writes in her book!   45
Oh happy he to find, whose hap shall be,
The deep channel of this swift running brook,
Whose name is life, that many wish to see.
Wretched and blind the common sort that stay
Their hope on things which time reaves in a trice,   50
All deaf, naked and subject to decay,
Quite void of reason and of good advice
And wretched mortal men throughout diseased.
Whose beck doth guide the world, by whom at jar
Are set the elements and eke appeased,   55
Whose skill doth stretch beyond my reach so far
That even the angels are content and joy
Of thousand parts but one to see, and bend
Their wits to this, and this wish to enjoy.
Oh happy wandering mind, aye hungering to the end,   60
What mean so many thoughts? One hour doth reave
That many years gathered with much ado.
Tomorrow, yesterday, morning and eve,
That press our soul and it encumber so,
Before him pass shade-like at once away,   65
For *was* or *shall be* no place shall be found
But for the time of *is, now* and *today,*
Only eternity knit fast and sound.
Huge hills shall be made plain that stopped clean
Our sight, nor shall there anything remain   70
Whereon may hope or our remembrance lean,
Whose change make other do that is but vain,
And life to seem a sport. Even with this thought,
What shall I be, what was I heretofore,
All shall be one nor piece-meal parted ought.   75
Summer shall be nor winter any more,

But time shall die, and place be changed withal,
And years shall bear no rule on mortal fame,
But his renown forever flourish shall
That once achieved to be of flowering name.   80
Oh happy souls that now the path doth tread
Or henceforth shall, when so it haps to be,
Which to the end whereof I speak doth lead.
Of fair and wandering sprights yet happiest she
Whom death hath slain far short of nature's bound.   85
The heavenly talk, good words and thoughts so chaste
Open shall lie unfolded in that stound,
Which kind within a youthful heart hath placed.

THE SECOND CHORUS FROM
SENECA'S *HERCULES OETAEUS*

What harming hurl of fortune's arm thou dreadest,
Let fraught of faith the burden of care relieve,
And take thou such, to fear approved by proof,
The unpicked locks of certain trust to hold;
For geason is the faith, and rarely kept is trust,   5
Where puffed sails from best forewinds be fallen.
The weight of scepter's sway if choice must bear,
Albeit the vulgar crew fill full thy gates,
And hundred thresholds with their feet be smoothed:
Though with thy gleaves and axes thou be armed,   10
And root full great do glory give thy name,
Amid the view of all these sundry sorts
One faultless faith her room even scant may claim.
The golden ledge full wrathful spites besets,
And where the gates their posts draw forth by breadth   15
More easy way to guiles and passed safe.
Heed then the clocks of warned harms with good,
And let the hidden blade not wrong thee work,
For when most show by gazers' eyes is spied,
And presence great thy honor most advance,   20
This gift retain as fellow to thy room:

Disdain may frown, but envy thrust thee through.
No ofter doth the east the night's care release
And makes the shady dark with light abash
Than kings be made in an instant short, and marred;   25
So icy is their joy and hopeless woe.
The love of kingdom's rule observed with care,
But for himself a king but few regard.
The court's luster a stale guest made for me,
Delighted with the shine no woe forthought.   30
And this man seeks the nearest room to prince,
To glittering view amid the streets he comes;
While broiled is with cark the miser's breast
In search of gainful grasp his name to spread.
In compass of the hoarded heaps to find   35
One bit to slake desire's wave he seeks.
Not all the coast where Istrus' trade doth haunt,
With gems bedecked through hue of diverse kind,
Nor Lydia fair with sweetest streams suffice
To quench nor answer all such thirst by half;   40
Nor yet the soil that bides Zephirus' slave,
Abashed at golden shining Tagus' beams,
Nor Hebrus' service may content at full,
Rich though Hydaspes' hedge his fields throw out,
Though Ganges' course his confines all do graze   45
With filled force to water all his lands.
To greedy grating wights enough not all
That nature well doth please his lack not so.
This man doth homage unto kingly force,
And harbor Rome adores where last he haunts,   50
Not meaning that this plowshare should advance
Like crooked hind his master's gain with clots
By murdering the ground; no ease of toil
Though thousand leas his husbandmen turn up.
Well pleased rests his hearth with goods even such   55
As pleasure may by gift another need.
A badder sort the prince's court regard
With foiled foot that stumble gives at all

And each to lose with no avail to one.
That might may equal harm they power achieve   60
Whose living's thread drawn out is of such length
Whom hap nor takes ere nature calls away.
The horned newed moon them blessed calls
Whose wane them misers judges when day doth fall.
A man full rarely happy is and old.   65
More surer sleeps thee downy turfs procure:
All Tyre, where purple woven is and made,
Not so sound slumber doth his owner yield.
The gilded roofs the quiet rest bereave,
And waking nights the purple draws from ease.   70
O that the breasts of rich men naked were,
The smoothed dreads of lofty lucks that hide;
The Brutian stream more milder course doth hold
When eastern wind him strikes with force's stroke.
In franched mind from care the silly soul possest,   75
A pot of beechen tree full sure he keeps
With steady hand that fears no snatch from hold.
No sudden fright affrays, no thief he dreads;
With ease y-got and single show he feeds
And recks not for the girded blades to thigh.   80
The golden cup of bloody mixture keeps.
The wife that is y-tied to man of mean estate
No carking hath in order pain to set,
Nor shining gift of reddy sea she wears
Her ears free from the pluck of gemmy weight;   85
No stone of Eoas' waves her cumber makes.
Soft wool ingrained with Sidon's purple fair
Drinks not the red for use that her befalls;
No Maeon needle filleth she with skeins
By parted hues that give the shade with art.   90
The silky land that lies to sunny east
Needs not the fruit from eastern tree to pluck;
Every herb the colors' die may mix
That distaff fills with yarn that skill not spun.
She nursed not the doubts of wedlock bed;   95
Of lewd suspect of weary works she shuns.

The wrathful lamp Erinis lighteth up
The feastful day adorns by pestering rout.
The poor man deemeth not his happy state
Till wealthy folk by fall it show.   100
Who so, therefore, the middle way eschews
The wry and crooked balk's most sure to tread.
While Phaeton boy one day of father got
To rule the reins and eke his wain to guide
In leaving wonted walk and worned ways   105
Which by slide, while the uncouth skies he shares
Such place as heat of Phoebus' flame knew not.
His ruin was the world his fellow plain.
Daedalus yet more larger scope and broader took,
Who never yet a sea by name did grace.   110
Though Icarus sought the true and living birds
By guile to pass and win the tryer's right,
His father's feathered wings despised with scorn,
To Phoebus near with swifty gait he hies,
And christened by this slip the sea was sure.   115
Evil bought the great where ill exceeds the good.
Let one full happy be and highly flee.
God shield that mighty me the vulgar call.
The lee of shore my silly boat shall loathe,
Let no full wind to depth my bark bequeath.   120
From safest creeks doth fortune glide and shun,
With search in middest sea for tallest ship
And takes its dearest prey the nearer to cloud.

THE METRES OF BOETHIUS'
CONSOLATION OF PHILOSOPHY

I.i.

Righmes that my groing studie ons perfourmed,
    In teares, alas, cumpeld, woful staves begin.
My muses torne, behold, what write I shuld, indites,
    Wher tru woful uerse my face with dole bedews.
Thes at lest no terror might constrain,   5

That felowes to our mone our way they shuld refrain.
The glory ons of happy griny youthe,
    Now, fates of grounting age, my comfort all.
Vnlookt for age hied by mishaps is come,
    And sorow bidz his time to add withal.   10
Vnseasond hore heares upon my hed ar powrd,
    And loosed skin in feable body shakes.
Blessed dethe, that in switest yeres refraines,
    But, oft calld, comes to the woful wights.
O with how defe eare she from the wretched wries,   15
    And wailing yees, cruel, to shut denies.
While gileful fortune with vading goodz did shine,
    My life wel ny the doleful houre bereved;
Whan her fals looke a cloude hath changed,
    My wretched life thankles abode protractz.   20
Why me so oft, my frendz, have you happy cald?
    Who fauleth downe in stedy step yet never stode.

I.ii.

O in how hedlong depth the drowned mind is dimme!
    And losing light her owne, to others darkenis drawne,
As oft as driuen with erthely flawes the harmful care
        upward grows.
    Wons this man fre in open fild used the skies to vew,
Of rose sun the light beheld,   5
    Of frosty mone the planetz saw,
And what star els runs her wonted cours.
    Bending by many circles this man had wone
By number to knowe them all;
    Yea, causis eache whens roring windz the seas perturbz.   10
Acquainted with the spirit that rolles the stedy world,
    And why the star that falz to the Hisperias waters
From his reddy roote doth raise herself.
    Who that gives the springes mild houres ther temper,
That with rosy floures the erthe be deckt,   15
    Who made the fertile autumne at fullist of the yere

Abound with grape al solne with ripest fruits.
   He, wonted to serche and find sondry causes of hiden
     nature,
Downe lies of minds light bereued,
   With brused neck by overheuy chaines,   20
A bowed lowe looke by waight bearing,
   Driven, alas, the sely erthe behold.

I.iii.

Than night overblowen, the darkenis left me,
   And formar strengh unto my yees retornd.
As whan the heavens astound with hedlong wind,
   And pale amidst the cloudy mistes
The sun is hid, and in the heavens no stars aperes,   5
   From hy the night on erthe is spred:
The same if Boreas sent from his Tracien den
   Doth strike and opens the hiden day,
Shines out, and with his soudan light Φebus shaken
   With his beams strikes al lokars on.   10

I.iv.

Who so quiet in setled life
   Proud fate kepes under fote
And stable defending eache fortune
   His chire unwonne preserues,
Him shal no rage nor seas threates,   5
   From depthe that hurles her fome,
Nor wood Veseuus with holy pittz
   That burstz out his smoky fires,
Nor way of flaming sulφar, wont to strike
   The towers hie, can moue.   10
Why so muche can wretched men
   At fiers tirants wondar, forsles, furious?
Hope thou naugh ne feare,
   Disarme thou may the powreles ire;
But who so quaking feares or wische,   15

Not being stable, and in his strengh
Down falz his shild, and changing place,
Huges the chaine by wiche he is drawen.

I.v.

O framar of the starry circle,
Who, lening to the lasting grounstone,
Withe whorling blast hevens turnest
And law compelst the skies to beare,
Now that with ful horne,   5
Meting all her brothers flames,
The lessar stars the mone dimmes,
Now darke and pale her horne,
Nar to the son loseth her light.
And she that at beginning of night   10
Hesperus frosen rising makes,
And Luciϕar palled by Φebus upriseth,
Againe her wonted raines exchangeth.
Thou, by the cold of lefe falne shade,
Straightist thy light with shortar abode,   15
Thou, when the feruent sommar comes,
Easy nights houres deuidest.
Thy power tempers the changing year,
That what leves Boreas blastz bereves
Gentil Seϕirus brings as fast: 20
Sedes that the north star doth behold
At highest blade the dok star burneth up.
Naught loused from auncient law
Leves the work of her owne place.
Al giding with assured end,   25
Man's works alone thou dost dispice,
O gidar by right desart from mean to kipe.
For why so many slipar fortune
Turnes doth make? Oppressing fautles
Dew paine for wicked mete,   30
But in hy seatz the wicked factz abide,
And wicked stamps on holy necks

With uniust turne,
And cleare uertu dimmed
With thick blackenis lurketh,   35
And iust man the wickeds crime doth beare.
Fals othe in fraude doth the annoy.
Who whan the can use ther forse,
Whom many uulgar feare,
The mightiest kings they can subdue.   40
O now behold of wretched rathe,
Thou who so ties the bondz of all;
Vs men regard, of thy great worke not the vilest part,
How tost we be with fortunes waues.
O weldar apeace the roring floudes   45
And with what boundz the great heauen thou gidest
The stable erthe do stedy.

I.vi.

Whan heuy Cancer sm^e
By Φebus beames inflames,
Than he that lent plentyes sead
To forowes that denied them,
Bigiled by Ceres faithe,   5
Let him seake the acorne tre.
The decked wode seake not
Whan thou violetz do gather,
Whan with the northy blastz
Ther roring fildz affrightz,   10
Nor seake not thou with gredy hand
The springy palmes to weld:
Grapes if thou wische injoy,
In autumne Bacchus rather
His gifts bestowes.   15
Times God assigneth fit
For eche mans office best,
Nor the tournes that he appoints
Suffers to be mixte.
So what so leues by rachelous way   20

The certain rule
Joyful ende shall neuer hit.

I.vii.

Dim cloudes,
Skie close
Light none
Can afourd.
If roling seas   5
Boustious sowth
Mixe his fome,
Griny ons
Like the clirristz
Days the water   10
Straight moude
Sturd up al foule
The sight gainsais.
Running stream
That poures   15
From hiest hilz
Oft is staid
By slaked
Stone of rock.
Thou, if thou wilt   20
In clirest light
The trothe behold,
By straight lin
Hit in the pathe.
Chase joyes,   25
Repulse feare,
Thrust out hope,
Woe not retaine.
Cloudy is the mind
With snafle bound   30
Wher they raigne.

II.i.

This whan her proud hand changeth cours
   And Euripus foming like is throwne,

Whilom she fierce kings cruel destroies,
   And lowe looke of won man deceitful raiseth.
She hereth not the wretche nor hedeth his teares,   5
   Willingly skornes the sighs that spitful she made.
Thus playeth she, and so her strength doth trie;
   A wondar great to hers she shewes:
If any man you view, one houre
   Both thrals him and   10
      Extolz.

II.ii.

If sandz such store by raging flawes
   As stured sea turnes up,
Or skies bidect with mighty stars
   The heuens al that lights,
And suche welthe bestowes,   5
   Nor plenty with fullist horne withdrawes her hand,
Mankind yet ceaseth not
   With wailing mones bewail him.
Thogh God his vowes willingly receue,
   The liberal dolar of golds plenty,   10
And gridy folke with honors great indues,
   Naught to haue got they seame,
But egar rauining, deuouring what they had,
   Stretcheth the chawes for more.
What raignes can drawe bak   15
   Hedlong desiar to stable end,
Whan thirst of getting inflames
   The flowing man with largist gifts?
No man thinkes him riche
   Who quaking mones belives a beggar.   20

II.iii.

In poole whan Φebus with reddy waine
   The light to spred begins,
The star dimed with flames opprissing
   Pales her whitty lookes.
Whan wood with Siφirus mildding blast   5
   Blusheth with the springing roses,

And cloudy sowthe his blustering blastes,
  Away from stauke the beauty goes.
Some time with calmy fayre the sea
  Void of waves doth run;   10
Oft boistrus tempestz the north
  With foming seas turnes up.
If rarely stedy be the worldz forme,
  If turnes so many hit makes,
Belive slippar mens luckes,   15
  Trust that sliding be ther goods.
Certain, and in eternal law is writ,
  Sure standeth naugh is made.

II.iv.

Who lasting wyl
  Wary settel seat,
And stable not of roring
  Eurus blastz ben won,
And careth skorne   5
  The waves of thretning sea,
Shuns soking sandes,
  And top of hiest mount.
One the froward southe
  With all his affrights,   10
The other loused refuse
  A hanging waight to beare.
Fleing perillous lot
  Of pleasantz seat,
On lowe stone remember   15
  Thy house sure to place.
Thogh wynd blowe,
  Myxing waters to botom,
Thou, happy plast in strengh
  Of quietz rampar,   20
Happy shalt live
  And smile at skies
    Wrathe.

II.v.

Happy to muche the formar age
   With faithful fild content,
Not lost by sluggy lust,
   That wonts the long fastz
To louse by son got acorne,   5
   That knew not Baccus giftz
With molten honey mixed
   Nor Serik shining fleece
With Tirius venom die.
   Sound slipes gave the grasse,   10
Ther drink the running streme,
   Shades gave the hiest pine.
The depth of sea they fadomd not,
   Nor wares chosen from fur
Made stranger find new shores.   15
   Than were navies stil,
Nor bloudshed by cruel hate
   Had fearful weapons staned.
What first fury to foes shuld
   Any army rayse   20
Whan cruel woundz he saw
   And no reward for bloude?
Wold God agane our formar time
   To wonted maners fel!
But gridy getting loue burnes   25
   Sorar than Etna with her flames.
O who the first man was
   Of hiden gold the waight
Or gemmes that willing lurkt
   The dear danger digd?   30

II.vi.

We know how many ruines made,
   Whan flamed citie and fathers slain,
That tirant who ons brother kild
   Imbrued with mothers bloude,

With looke oueruewed her body cold.   5
   No teares bedewes his face, but was
A domar of dedded beauty.
   The same yet with sceptar peple ruled,
Evin suche as son espies at furdest west
   From the orison come,   10
Whom frosty seven stars ouerlookes,
   Whom wrothful north with drie heat
Affraies in sithing of the burning sandz.
   Could all his lofty power at lenghe
Turne the rage of frantique Nero?   15
O grevous hap whan wicked sword
To cruel venom joingnes!

II.vii.

Who so with hedlong mynd glory
   Alone belives as greatest thing,
And quarters of largist hevens behold
   With straightid seat of erthe,
Wyl blusche that hit not filz   5
   The short compas of gridy desire.
Why, proud men, do you crake
   Your necks from mortal yoke retire?
Thogh fame by people strange
   Flying spred the tonges open,   10
And noble house by great titelz shine,
   Death hates the hiest glory,
Intangles low and hauty hed
   And equalz lest to most.
Wher now lies faithful Fabritius bones?   15
   Wher Brutus or currish Cato?
Small lasting fame signes
   A vaine name with fewest letters.
But why do we know noble names,
   Do we not see them to consumed?   20
Ly you shal unknowen at all,

Nor fame shal uttar who.
If you suppose that life be longar drawen
   For brethe of mortal fame,
Than the second dethe exspect.

II.viii.

That world with stable trust
   The changing seasons turnes
And divers sedes stil holdes league,
   That Φebus the ruddy daye
With golden car bringes furthe,   5
   That mone may rule the night
   Wiche Hesperus broght,
The gridy sea her streame
   In certaine limites kipt,
That lawful be not to wide world   10
   To bancke her spatius boundz:
Al this hole molde ties
   In ruling erthe and sea
Loue ruling hevens.
   Who if the raines he slake,   15
What so now by loue is linked
   Straict maketh war
And seakes to wracke that worke
   Whiche linked faithe
   Hit quiet motions moued.   20
He in holy peace doth hold
   The bounded peoples pact,
And linkes sacred wedlok
   With chast goodwyl,
Who lawes his owne   25
   To true associates giues.
O happy humain kind,
   If loue your mindz
The same that heuen doth rule
   Mygh gide.   30

III.i.

Who frutfulst fild wyl sowe,
    First fried of fruit must he make his leas,
With sithe must fern and busches cut,
    That Ceres may swel with new sede.
The flies labor swetar is,   5
    If strongar tast be first eate.
As Luciφar dothe the darkenis chase,
    A fayre day spurs on the ruddy hors.
Thou, looking so on falsed good,
    Begin thy neck from yoke to pluck.   10
Therby thy mind may true obtain.

III.ii.

How many raines of causis gideth
    Nature powreful, by which the great
World with lawes provident kepes
    And tijnge, strains with unlousing
Knot eche thing, wel pleases with shirllest   5
    Note expres with drawing strings.
Thogh Aφricke lionnes faire
    Gives beare and takes giuen food with paw
And cruel kipar feares the wonted stripes that bare;
    If bloud haue ons dyed ther looke   10
Ther courage retournes to formar state,
    And with rorings lowde them selues remembring,
Slacks from tied knots ther necks,
    And furius first with cruel tothe
On kipar raging wrathe bestowes.   15
    The chatting bird that sings on hiest bow,
In holow den is shut is she.
    To this, thogh cups with hony lined
And largest food with tendar loue
    Beguiling care of man bestowes,   20
If yet skipping on the eues
    Spies pleasing shady wood,
With fote she treds her skatterd meat,

In sorowing seakes the woodz alone,
And with swit vois the trees resountz.   25
   The twig drawen ons with mighty fors
Bowing plies her top;
   The same if bending hand do slack,
The top upright doth turne.
   The son to Hesperius waters falz,   30
But by secret pathe againe
   His cart turnes to est againe.
Each thing sekes owt his propre cours
   And do reiois at retourne ther owen,
Nor ordar giuen to any remains   35
   Onles he joinges to end his first
And so stedyes his holie round.

III.iii.

Thogh riche man with flowing golden golfe
   Couetous hepes not rechis that suffice,
His neck adornes with geme of reddis sea,
   With hundred oxe the fruitful fildz doth til,
Yet eating care leues him not quicke,   5
   Nor ded the fliting good accompagnies.

III.iv.

Thogh the proude man with Tirius shelles
   Be dekt and shining stone,
Hated yet of all liued Nero
   For cruel lust.
But ons thogh wicked he gaue   5
   Vnmete curules to reuerent fathers.
Who yet happy thoght them
Whom wicketz sort estemed?

III.v.

He that sekes mighty be,
   Cruel myndz must tame,
Nor won with lust his neck

Filthy raynes subdue.
Thogh India soil far of   5
  At thy lawes do shake,
And uttermost island
  Serue the to,
Yet is hit not thy powre
  Hiden cares expel,   10
Nor wretched mones
  Expulse thou canst not.

III.vi.

Al humain kind on erthe
  From like beginninge comes:
One father is of all,
  One only al doth gide.
He gaue to son the beames   5
  And hornes on mone bestowed,
He men to erthe did giue
  And signes to heauen.
He closed in limmes our soules
  Fetched from hiest seat.   10
A noble sede therfor broght furth
  All mortal folke.
What crake you of your stock
  Or forfathers old?
If your first spring and auther   15
  God you view,
No man bastard be,
  Vnless with vice the worst he fede
And leueth so his birthe.

III.vii.

All delight hathe this with hit,
  With stinge in joyars hit
Like to winged flies,
  Whan hony the haue made,
Away the go and with stikking   5
Bite, the stinged hartes strikes.

III.viii.

O in how begiling pathe
  Men ignorance leades.
Seake not the golde in griny tre
  Nor look for precious stone on grape;
Hide not on hily tops your baites   5
  Your dische with fische to fil,
And gotes if thou wylt take
  The tyrrhene sea not serche.
For hid in the waues man knoes the waters stream,
And what fiersist riuer haue whittist pearle,   10
  Or wher the reddys rubies
And shores also fild most with smallist fische
  Or haue most porpos skales.
But hiden for they know not
  The good the seake,   15
Blindid ignorant must the bide
  To cerche byonde the northen pole,
Drowned in the erthe the rake.
  What hest shall I for dullardz make?
Euen this, that whan with carke the falz haue got,   20
Truist than shalt knowe
    The best.

III.ix.

O thou in lasting sort the world that rulest,
Of erthe and heauen the framar, who time from first
Bidst go and stable stedy all elz dost while,
Whom outward causis forst not to forme
The worke of sliding substance, but shape   5
Of greatest good that envy wantz, thou al
By hiest sample gides: the fairest thou,
The goodlist world that mindst, and of like mold hit
    made,
Bidding the perfaictz the complete parts performe.
In number thou elementz ties, as ryming cold   10
To melting flames be ioingned: lest purest fire faile

Or waights to drowned land befall.
Thou binding the soules spirite the moues
Al that concernes the triple nature
And dost deuide them into agrying limmes.   15
Who cut in circles two the motion glimmers,
And brething to her selfe retournes
The dipe mind bisetz and alike heauin rules.
Thou with like cause the soules consernes
And liues that meanar be to swiftist wains,   20
Thou fitting hiest spirites
In heauen and erthe dost sowe,
Whom with a gentil law to the retourned
Thou makest be broght to fire from whence it came.
Grant that the mynd, O father, climb to thy hiest seat.   25
And on thy vew the clirest sigh may set.
Away cast erthely cloude and waight of this mold,
Do thou with lustar then them grace.
Thou art the cleare and quiet rest for best folke,
The to admire is first, last, help, gide,   30
    Pathe and stedy last.

III.x.

Al you togither come that taken be,
Whom begiling lust with wicked chanes hath bound,
Dabeling the erthely myndz;
Here rest of labor shal you haue,
Here open sanctuary for wretches alone.   5
Not al that Tagus with her golden sandz
Doth give, or Hermus with her glittering shore,
Or Indian dwelling nire to hottische circle,
That griny stone with clirist doth mixe,
So clires the sight, nor more the blindid mindz   10
Returnes into ther shades.
What of al thes hathe pleased and delited,
   That erthe hathe kept in darkist caue:
The lustar that doth gide the heauen and rule,
   The ruines dark of soule forbidz.   15

This light he who can decerne
Beauty suche in Φebus beames denies.

III.xi.

Who so the trueth with deapest mynd doth sirche
And sekes by no bywais awry to stray,
Into him selfe returne the light of newar mynd,
And longe discours straining to a round,
And teach his mynd what so without he seke,   5
Layd up amonge his treasure let him kepe.
Lately that which blacky cloud hathe dimmed,
That lightar shal thou shine out.
For not al light from mynd hath drawen
The body carying a forgetful waight.   10
Ther stiks, I trowe, an inward sead of trothe
Wiche kindlez best by learnings belowes.
For axed why do you the right desire,
If instinct in thy hart ther wer not?
If Platoes musis tales the trueth,   15
That eche man lernes
Forgetting he remembars.

III.xii.

Blist that may of good
The fontane clire behold,
Happy that can of waighty
Erthe the bondes to breake.
The Tracian profit wons   5
His wives funeralz wailing
Whan with sorows note
The wauering trees he moued,
And stedy rivers made,
And hind caused join   10
Unfearing sides to lion fierce,
Nor hare did feare the looke
Of cruel dog so plised with song.
Whan ferventar desir the inward

Brest more burnt,   15
Nor could the notes that al subdued
Pacifie ther lord,
Of ireful gods complaining,
The helly house went to.
Ther faining verse,   20
Tuning to sounding stringe
What he drew from springes
The greatest of mother gods,
What feable mone could giue,
What doubled love afourd,   25
Bywailes and hel doth stur
With dulce suite pardon
Of darkenes lord besiche.
Wondar doth the thre hedded
Jailor, amasid with unwonted verse;   30
Revenging goddes of faultes
That wontid guilty feare,
Sorowing with tears bedewed the were.
Not Ixiones hed
The whirling while did turne,   35
And lost with longue thirst
Tantalus riuers skornes.
The vultur fild with notes
Tityus livor tared not.
At last wailing said the juge   40
Of shady place: We yield;
To man we giue his wife for feere,
Won by his song.
With this law bound be the gift,
While in Tartar thou bidest   45
Turne back thy looke thou must not.
But who to loue giues law?
For greatest law his love he made.
So, night drawing to her ende,
Eurydicen his Orφeus   50
Sawe, lost and killed.

This fable toucheth you,
Who so doth seak to gide
To hiest day his mynd.
For who in hely shade   55
Won man his yees doth bend,
What so he chifest held
In vewing hel hathe lost.
        Et sic bene.

IV.i.

For spedy quilles haue I
    That fur aboue the pole do reache,
Wiche whan my fliinge mind putz on,
    Hating the erthe despice hit.
And hiar hies than erthes globe,   5
    And cloudes behind me see,
And pas aboue the fiars top
    With swiftnis that the heavens heat,
Until to starry house hit comme
    With Φebus sorteth way,   10
And soldiar made of shining star
    Cold Saturne doth felowe,
    Or wher the shewing night
The circle round doth make.
    And whan got ynough she hathe,   15
The owtmost pole he leues,
    And worthy made of hiest light
Presseth the waight of spidy skie.
    He, lord, holdz of kings the septar
    And raines of world doth gide,   20
And stable rules the spidy cours,
    Of all the noble juge.
Hither if the way back do bring the,
    Wiche now forgetting thou requirest:
This, wilt thou say, my country is, I know.   25
    Hens came I, hire wyl I stay my step.
And if of erthe hit plese the

The darkenes left to vewe,
The grimme lookis that people dredeth so
    Of banissed tirants shalt behold.   30

IV.ii.

Thos wiche you se as kings
    Sit in ye top of hiest seat,
Florishing with purple fayre,
    Invirond with dreadful armes,
With ireful looke that thretes,   5
    For hartz yre scant drawing brethe.
If any take from wicked men
    Of false honor the couer,
Within shal se ther lordz
    Straightened giues to beare.   10
Hither lust them drawes,
    Hire ire ther myndz afflictz,
Who sturred raiseth stormes,
    Sorow or the taken wers,
Or slippar hopes tourment.   15
    Wherfor whan one hed
So many tirantz beares,
    He doth not that he wold,
    Prest with so wicked lordz.

IV.iii.

Ulisses captaines sailes
And sailing ships in sea
Eurus to iland broght.
The goddis feare sitting,
As borne of Φebus line,   5
To her newe gestz
The charmed cup doth giue.
Wiche as in divers sortz
Herber rular gides her hand,
This man the bores snout do couer,   10
Another the Marmican lion

With tuske and paw indueth.
This like to the wolfe nv borne,
Whan wepe he wolde, he houles.
Another as Indian tigar   15
Walkes in his house as mild.
Thogh from many euelz
The winged Arcadian god
Pitying the besiged captaine
From gestz plague preserved,   20
Yet wicked cup the sailars
With mouthes supte up,
And swin changed Ceres corne
For foode of acorne chosen.
Of lost men naught remained   25
Of body or of voyce.
Only ther mynd stable aboue
Whan the monstars suffar, wailes.
O hand to weke nor herbes of power,
Thogh limmes to change,   30
Hartz yet alter may not.
Whithein bides men strengh,
Hid in his towre.
Thos venoms with more fors
Man from himselfe withdrawes,   35
Who, thogh the body not,
The soule with woundz assailes.

IV.iv.

What boutes hit make so great strife
  And with thy hand thy dethe procure?
If dethe you seake, she draweth ny
  Agreyng, not abides the winged horse.
Whom serpent, lion, tigar, beare and bore   5
  With bite do seake, with blade your selues pursue.
That properties agre not but do difar,
  Ar they the cause of wicked strife and war,
And perish wold with weapon diuers?

No just meane of cruelty ynough.   10
Fit mede woldest thou giue desartz?
  Of right the good do loue, the yl bemone.

IV.v.

If man know not how stars
The Arcture next by hyest poles doe slyde,
Nor why Bootes slow glydes by yᵉ wane
And sluggy flames in sea doo dip,
When her swift rysings to soone performs,   5
Of hyest heauens the law will muse.
Of fulled moone the hornes whitenid
Infected with yᵉ bounds of darkest night.
And such as with her shyning face were shaded
Dymmed Pheba those stars discouer;   10
A common error folkes assayles,
And brasen tymbrells stryke with many strokes.
None musith that the southest wynd
With hurling waue astones the shore,
Nor that yᵉ hardnid snowy ball by cold   15
By feruent heate of sonne resolues.
For ready is the cause of yˡˢ be seene,
But hydden causes whyrls yᵉ mynd.
Such as our age scarce knowith lyke
And vulgar fleete at souden gase.   20
Let cloudy faulte of error giue his place
And wonders sure be seene shall cease.

IV.vi.

If wary alone of thundering God yᵉ lawes thou wilt
With purest mynde beholde,
Of hyest heauen the top doe vewe.
There planets, with justest league of all,
Agreement old doo kepe.   5
The sonne, styrd up by ruddy fyre,
Phebas frosy axill tree ne letts,
Nor that beare that on yᵉ top of the world

A running course doth bend,
That neuer other stars wet beholding 10
Dround under western depth is touched,
And seketh not with flames the sea to hit.
Ever with equall turne of tyme
Hesperus showes yᵉ later shades,
And Lucifer retournes yᵉ fayrest day. 15
So interlaced looue renewes
The eternall courses all,
So jarring warr from starry sky made outlaw.
The elementz all accord tempars
In equal sort, that striving 20
Moisteurs to droughts [by] turnes giue way,
That the coldz kipe faithe with flames,
And hanging fire upward bend.
And heuy erthe with waight bow downe.
By seluesame cause in milddist springe 25
The flowring yere his sauors yeldz,
Hottist sommer corne doth ripe,
And fruitful autumne apples beares,
Dripping showres wintar moistz.
This temper feedes and brings fourth 30
What so lyfe in world doth brethe.
The same snatching makes and plucks away
By the last gasp ending spring.
The maker hye meane while sitts,
Ruling bends of all yᵉ raynes, 35
King and lord, spring and first
Lawe, and wise, of just yᵉ judge,
And such by styrring as he rayses,
Backdrawing stayes, and wandring keeps.
For but returning rightest lynes 40
Again he bent to bowing wheels
The order that now stable keeps
Disseuerd all from spring wold faynte.
Such is yᵉ common loue of all,
That with returne, for end of good be kept. 45

In other sort endure they could not,
Unles agayne by loue returnd
Back to the cause that made them bend.

IV.vii.

Twis fiue yeres wratheful Atride made
With Φrisians ruines war,
The unchast bed of brother so revenged.
He, while hoissing sailes to Grecians ship he gaue,
With wische and bloud the windes apeced;   5
Dispoiled of fathers care, the cruel priest
His daughtars throte of life deprived.
Vlysses wailed his lost peers
Whom bloudy Poleφemus in his large den
Gulped down unto his cruel panche,   10
And furius yet with his yeles hed
His joy repaid with woful teares his owne.
Hardy labors his Hercules did grace.
He centaurs proude did tame,
Of skin the lion flead,   15
With certain shaftes the birdz did hit,
Snatched aples from the looking dragon,
His left hand peaced with golden metal,
Cerberus with threfold cheane doth drawe.
A victor he is said to set the lord for meat   20
To cruel forefoted bests.
Hidra killed by venom sered,
Achelous streame with firy looke
Drowned under the shore his shamed face.
Anteus he strake undar the Libeans sandes,   25
Cacus apesed Euanndars wrothe
And shuldars those wiche by heauens shuld pres
The bore the same with folme did marke.
The last labor heauen beareing with nek unboued
The heauen decernes for labors pane.   30
Forward go that stronge be wher hiest way
Of graetest sample bides.

Why, sluggardz, baks do you tourne?
The erthe won, the heauens he
    Giues.

V.i.

Near the craggs of Achemians rock wher turned to
    folowars
Brests the flying warior dartz doth throw,
From one springe Tigris eke Euφrates arise,
Strait by waters parted soundred be;
Who met and in one cours reclaimed,   5
The streame that eache depthe drew agries.
Let top sailes meet and trunckis by currant drawen
And mixed waters fil the changing cours,
And suche falz as bending erthe hath skattered
A running ordar of falling gulfe ordars.   10
So what so seame by slakning ranes to slip
Chanchis bit yet indures and by a law goes on.

V.ii.

Cleere Phebus with purest light
The honnyed mouth of Homer sings.
Who yet yᵉ deepe bowells of earth and sea
With weake sight of beames pears not,
Not so of the great world the framar.   5
Gainst him that al from hy doth view
No waight of erthe may resist,
Not night with darkist clouds ganesays.
In moment stroke his mynd all sees,
What wer, what be, what shal bifall,   10
Whom sole alone for that he al espies
Truly the may sole call.

V.iii.

What disagrijng cause the bond of all things breakes?
What god suche wars twixt two trothes makes,
That what so coupled singly agree

The selfsame mixt must be disionyed?
But discord none among the truthes befals,   5
And certain sure vnto themselues do stik?
But mynd opprest by blindid limmes
Can not by flame of overwhelmed light
The smal knots of al things finde.
But why with suche desire doth true mynde seake   10
The hiden causes of thinges serche out?
Knowes he that gridely to knowe he wyls?
Why strives he to knowe agane the had?
If ignorant he be, why blindid things seakes he?
For who that wischeth that knowes not what,   15
Or who foloweth that he wots not?
Or how may he finde, or found knowe
Suche forme of wiche he knowes not shape?
And whan he viewes the hyest mynd,
The chief and al togither may he get?   20
But now the mynd, hid in limmes cloudes,
Hath not of al forgot his owne,
And, thogh the partz be lost, retaines the hed.
Who euer seakes the trueth to knowe,
Of nether sort is rightly called,   25
For nether al doth knowe or ignorant of al,
But top of al retaining kipes by whose aduis,
From hy the seen draweth that bettar he may
The partz forgot the kept rejoingne.

V.iv.

Ons in the porch wer broght in men
Of obscure line, and old the wer,
Who sens and image out of lest motes
In mens myndz ingrauen beliue,
As oft haps the running stile   5
In sea paper leue,
Some printid lettars stik,
That marke haue none at all.
But if the mynd by her owne raigning

Expris by motions naught,   10
Saue only patient lies
Subiiect to bodies markes
And vain the fourmes
Glaslike of all doth make.
Whenche this that in our mynd raignes   15
Knoweledge of al discernes?
What power al beholdz,
Who the knowen deuides?
And knowing eache way
Now lifts on hie the hed,   20
Than falz to lowest thinges,
Than gathering in hit selfe
With truethe fals rebukes?
This is the making cause
Wiche much more mightiar is   25
Than suche as only material markes
Receaues with her owne prints.
But yet a passion doth begin and sturs
The myndz fors while body liues,
Whan ether light the yees doth hit,   30
Or sound in ear doth strike.
Than sturred strengh of mynd
What figures within hit holds
Joigned like he cals,
Applies them to the outward knowen,   35
And fancies mixe to formes
That hiden rest within.

V.v.

In how many shapes pas beastes on ground,
Of wiche of bodies long the dust some turnes
With fors of brest contin[u]ed trace doth trail,
Some whos swiftnis wings the windz do part
And strait the bredhth of largist skie doth pas,   5
Some on ground ther steps to print reiois,
Or griny fildz to pas, or woodz to haunt.

Whos formes thogh thou see difar far,
Yet downe face thers ther dullid sencis.
Mankind alone his hed upward bendz,   10
At eas doth stand with body clad and erthe lookes on.
This figure warns, but for the clays deceat,
That thou with liftid looke that heauen aspiring upcast
    thy he[d],
On hy thy mynd shuldst raise, lest overwaid
Thy body made aloft, thy mynd shuld   15
       Lowar sit.

HORACE'S *ART OF POETRY*
(LINES 1–178)

If to a mans hed a pantar wold
  A horsis neck conjoine
And coulored fethers ad therto
  With limmes togither set,
That face aboue of woman faire,   5
  The rest fowle like the moudy fische;
For suche a hap, my frindz,
  Could you your laughtar kipe?
Belive me, Pisons, euen to this tablet
  That my book be like,   10
Whos vane shapis shalbe faned,
  As sik mans dreames be wont,
So as nor fote ne hed in one agrie.
  An iniud power bold the poet and the pantar had.
We knowe this lein, axe and giue the same.   15
  Not so the wild and tame do pere,
Nor of the birdz that serpent bride,
  Nor lambes fal from tigres tetes.
Oft to beginnings graue and shewes of great is sowed
  A purple pace, one or more for vewe,   20
Whan wood or aultar Dians aught be drawen,
  Or crake of running streames in fairest fildz,
Than pant the riuer Rene or rainbow seak,

But for al thes hire is no place.
You can perchance the cipers trie present,   25
   What botes to pant for gayne a foteles man
From broken kile to swim to shore.
   A pot ful large was ment be maid:
How hapned than the while a pipkin framed?
   In time let be what so thou wilst   30
So that hit plain and one remain.
Of poets greatist part, O father, and youthes worthy of your
   sire,
   All be begiled by shewe alone of good.
While brife to be I striue, skars understode I am,
   And treting maters slite, I feale my strengh decay;   35
Professing causis dipe, my shalowe mynd astons,
   And criping low on ground, to safe yet fearing flawe.
Who so one thing expres in to to many sortes,
   A dolφin on the tries doth hange and bore in streame.
So flight from fault fals into lack from want of art.   40
   A sely smith in Emilius stage play in bras
Wil nailes and silky heare with his pensel shape.
   Vnhappy man in chifist part of worke,
For wanting of skil to pictur all he cannot.
   Self same am I, if aught I striue compound,   45
No more I wische than wondar of iuel formed nose,
   Or vew of blackist yee with here of likist hue.
Take you that write a matter suche as equalz best your skil
   And long do pause on what your shuldars doe refuse
Or what the beare may best: who that he chuse best under-
   stands,   50
   Nor eloquence shal he want nor ordar cleare.
For grace and vertu shal he place, or forbeare,
   So as what now be said or what hirafter shal
Much he defars and for the present time omitz.
   This loue he doth, this skorne of promised vers the skribe.   55
In placing wordz, if thou be skant and wary bothe,
   The spiche shal florische wel and be estimed.
Yea, if a new word for old wel sodered thou do place,

Yea, and nide be with new shewe the hiden yore expound,
To frame may hap some wordz that girdled Cethes lack,   60
  A license thou with shamfest leue mast take.
The new made wordes and faned like credit beares,
  If from the Grikis spring the softly be withdrawen.
But Romane what to Plauto and Cicilius shal he giue,
  If from Varios loue or Virgil hit be caught?   65
Why, if I litel get, nide enuid I to be,
  Whan Caton and Ennius toung inriched ther weany spiche,
And new names to ther matters gaue?
  Hit lawful is and euer shal, a word assigned by mark to
    know.
As primar leues of wood first faule and chaunge to nirest yere,   70
  So eldred age of wordz turnes so to ther decay,
And youngmen like the borne first florische and increas.
  To dethe we owe ourselves and all we haue.
Whether Neptune by erthe receued,
  And baying in by northern winde the sailing ships,   75
Wiche is a worke and act for kinge;
  Or wither a coustumed marische fit for ores
Fede the cities nire and makes them feale the plowes waight,
  Or streame change the cours, the fo to frutes,
By learning bettar way. All mortal dede shal end,   80
  Nor shal our wordz knowe honor augh nor liveliste grace.
Much shal renue that haue bine fallen, and than decay
  Suche wordz as haue bine reuerenst wel, if vse hit grant,
On whose beck bothe fors and fourme of spiche dependz.
  How kingz and chiftanes actz and eke ther doleful woe,   85
In verse how the in numbar be exprest Homere hath told.
  With onjvend linked vers at first a mone the make,
But after winning wische ther verdit the haue won.
  What author yet wil simple eglogs leue,
The grammars mastars striue, yet iuge the verdit kipes.   90
  Rage with his owne stile Archilocas hath used.
This manner vers the comidantz and tragike bothe begun
  Wel fitting wordz for bothe, exciding vulgar shoutes
And mitist for the greatist, waightist cause.

Our muse comitz to stringe bothe gods and ther race,   95
The winning wrastlar, and hors the first at stop,
    And telz the youngmens cares and frechat wines,
Thes changes to obserue and coulors shewed of work.
    If I knowe not nor care, why poete am I called?
By sely shame chuse not to knowe than sike vs lerne.   100
    A mery play wold not admit a tragik vers;
Thiestes scene disdaines that wordiest vers decerns,
    Be told in menar verse by pourist comidant.
Let all things be as sorteth best ther place.
    Yet comedie sometime lifts vp the voice,   105
And wrotheful Cremes with puffed face fights,
    And tragik often moues in slavy gise.
Teleφus, eke Pelius, wh[en] poore and exul bothe,
    Away throw the thes windblowen vase
And halved quartered vers, do care,   110
    If care the do, with mone the loukars on to move.
Versis faire do not suffice, let them be swite
    And suche as wher the wyl may turne the hirars eare.
As mery man the please, so wailing man contentz
    The milddy lookes. If teares myne thou procure   115
Thyself must waile, so shal thy misfortune yerk me.
    Ivel if you do your biddings place,
Teleφus or Peleus, or I shal slipe or laughtar make.
    For sory wordes fitz best a moning face,
The furius thretful, seuere the dalear, wanton the graue,   120
    For nature first us fourmed within ful fit,
For the bent of eche fortune helpes or throwes to er[the],
    In yrking drawes vs downe with wo opprest,
Strait motions of the minde exaltz by toung exprest.
    If speakars wordz unfit ther fate,   125
The army all with skorne wil the deride;
    For much hit doth auaill whir Dauus or Eros,
Or ripid age or firs youthe in growing yeres,
    Or ruling dame or careful nurse,
Wayfaring marchant, or plower of the griny fild,   130
    In Colchis or Assyria bred, in Thebes or Argus town.

Or hiresay folowe, or writar, make thy matter fit for the.
 Laudid Achilles do thou prais, hedy, ireful, graue, lerne
  [shipp].
Lawes he denies euer made for him, naugh must gainsay thy
  armes fors.
 Medea let be woode vnwon, Ino ful of teares,   135
Faithless Ixion, wandringe Io, mourning Orestes.
 If ignorant thou aught to the scene committ,
And darest new actors place perfourme,
 Suche as thou first began, louke to the end thou kipe.
Ful hard hit in private sort the comme thing declare,   140
 And rightliar shuldst thou Homers vers expres,
Than as first man the vntouche and vntold tel.
 General mattar shal be made thy private part,
If thou stik not to curius about the base and commen lines,
 Nor word by other like glosar sure shalt thou vse,   145
Nor skolar like shalt thou sample thyself in act,
 Whence shame forbidz thy foote eke lawe of work,
Nor so begin as Ciclicus writar ons:
 The luk of Priam shal I sing and worthy war.
What fitting so wiede chawes hathe promis now perfourned? 150
 The hilz ther frute do yeld, a skorned mouse is born.
How rightliar he that fondly naught doth vndertake.
 Shew me, my muse, a man in after tims of taken Troy
The manars of many a man that saw togither with their
  towns.
 Who miss not smoke of flame but light from smoke to
  giue,   155
That thens he may shewe wondars great:
 Antiфaton, Silla, and with Ciclop Caribid.
Nor Diomedz return from Meleagris ruine,
 Nor Trojans war from his grandfathers shel wil tel.
Euer to end he hies and to best menes.   160
 Like as by notes the listenars eares he drawes,
That he despaires, intreting grace, he leues;
 And so begiles as fals with tru doth mixe,
That midst to first and last with midst agrie.
 Thou, what I and people desire do, hire.   165

If nide you do a praisar, to the end such as wil bide
    Til singar do afourd your clapping hands to work,
Than must thou maike the manars of eche age,
    And graunted must be grace to natures changed yeare.
The boy that can pronounce his wordz   170
    And stedy his ground with sure pace
Lips for joy to felowe his like,
    Sturs vp his color, lets hit light fal,
And changes oft in many a houre.
    The berdles youthe, at last mastar cast of,   175
Joys in horsis, dogges, and gras of open fild;
    Waxlike rolled to vice, to teachar curst,
Late forsear of good, of his pence to lavische,
    Hauty, glorius, swift winged to leue that he loved.
But eldar age, turning his cours with mynd manlike,   180
    Riches sikes, frindz, to honor himself ingrafing,
Wel warning to do that strait to change he strives.
    Cumbars many a one besige the aged man;
Or that he sikes thogh found as wretche he forbears
    And dares not ventur the vse therof;   185
Or that in feare or yoy al thing he vndertakz,
    Slowghful a hoper, ydel, and gridy of change,
Crabbid, whining, the praisar of passed time
    Whan boy he was, a juge and beatar of his youngar.
Growing yeres great auailes do bring,   190
    And passed gone as many do deprive.
Lest, therfor, agid part be giuen vnto the young
    And mans estate bequived to the boy,
Let vs abide in suche as best agre and in ther time.

PLUTARCH'S *ON CURIOSITY*

[I] ·

Perchance hit might be best to shun at al that home
    Wher throughout the wind passage none can get,
Or dimmed darke or subiect to the cold and windz,
    Or els to siknis thral that bredeth helth decay;
But if so one delight by costom in such place   5

The lights may changed be, or staiers alter case,
Or dores some for the passage, some other shutted be,
    Wiche fayrar muche may frame hit cleare with bettar
    helth.
And some have served ther cities turne by altering suche.
    A sample may my country make, as said hit is,   10
That bending to Zephirus wynde and from Parnasus taking
    sone,
    That to yᵉ west his course did turn by Cherons help,
Hit wryed was to east, the sons arising place.
    Empedocles eke, the knower wel of naturs cours,
Is said to stop the gaping deap of hil and the rok   15
    Wiche grevous was and siknys ful the place,
For that the northen wind did beat on neagbours filds,
    And thus the plage out chast from regions ground.
Therfor if plagy wilz ther be that noyful ar unsound,
    Arising tempest great and dimly marks the mynd,   20
Best shal hit be giue them repuls and down throw flat to
    ground;
    So to ourselues we bride an air clear, a ligh and brethe ful
    pur.
And if this may not be, yet let our labor at lest be this,
    That by al menes that possible make we may,
Tourning from us and changing al [that] brideth us offence,   25
    We make them serue our tourne and helpe us the beste.
A sample let us make of curius nideles care,
    Whose study is naugh else but other homes to knowe,
Diseas that nether void of enuy nor pure from wickedn[is].
    Why than, O man, with enuye ful an others yls   30
Sharpist sight dost set, and in thyn owin stil?
    Inward drawe thy science study and so hit apply
That thy busy care be tourned from outward to thyn own.
    And if thou fancy haue to enter storyes yvels,
Thou hast ynough at home that ydel thou ne be.   35
        As great a stream as waters floud doth bring to bay,
        Or circled oak by fawling leves from tre.

So great a store of faultes in thy life shalt find,
A hepe eake of yl desiars fraught in thy mynd.
  No les neglect of that thou shuld by office yeld.   40
For as the writ of Senoφon telz the ordar how good frugal
    men
  Do part aside suche laid up stuf as sacrifice nides,
And do deuide from banquetz cost, in sort that some
  Do serue the plowshares turne, in other place the war;
Euen so do thou deuide thy ivels part that enuy bridz,   45
  A part let ielosy haue, some for cowardz frute do leue,
For sparing some, reserue all the do count and know.
  Suche windowes as to neghbours hous giues the vewe,
And curius foote steps make a way to patent;
  But other wayes open thou must, truly fit and sound,   50
Suche as to seruauntz romes in thy hous the bring,
  Sometime into thy womens closetz and wher thy slaues
    abide.
Thes be suche thing as axing study and busy care do nide,
  Wher never profitles businis nor wicked work hath rome,
But ful of welth and holesum councel giues the,   55
  Whan eache telz himself this tale and this accompt:
Whens slide I, what done haue I, what ther vndon shuld not?

[2]

But now, as fables tell, Lamia at home doth blindedly:
  Her yees she putz in vesselz store til furthe she go.
Than in her hed the go, and open bendz her lookes.
  So eache man abrode in others matters with hate
  Into his thoght a curius regard into his head as yee he putz.   5
From faultz our owne and wicked actz by ignorance we slip;
  On thes nor rolling yees nor light of them receue.
The curius more profit yeldz his foes than good vnto himself,
  That telleth them ther lacks, and wher the do, and
That bettar the may ware the warnid to correct,   10
  Neglectz at home the dedes that nide wer to regard,
So stoned is his care for that most other touche.

Vlisses eke no word wold giue to mother his
Til of the proφet axed he had the cause, why to hel he went;
 And after he to dame returned and wemen rather axed 15
What wenche Tiro was, wher faire Cloris bid,
 And what bred cause for murthering Epicastes life,
  Whan woful knot of corde she knitz to hiest beame.
But we ouer secure and knowing naugh that most us touche,
 Inquires of others liues: as why our neghbors sire 20
A Sirian was and grand dame why a Thresian borne,
 And suche man owes talentz thre nor usury hath paid.
Yea, and sometime suche things discours, whens suche a wife
 leaue home,
 Why he and he haue in a corner talkt togither.
But Socrates romed up and downe with doute ful great, 25
 What wordz, what spiche Pitagoras vsid to bride belife;
And Aristippus in Olimpias meting Ischomachus axed
 Why Socrates in his disputes so wyn could yonge men.
Who whan he picked had some sedes and samples of his
 wordz,
 So moued he was, that skant he stedy cold his pas, 30
And grew throughout bothe pale and lene, until
 Thirsty and inflamed to Athenes hoissed vp his sailes,
And bothe the man his wordz and φiloφie he lerned,
 Wiche did contain in somme to all conclude in short
That al men shuld an audit make of al ther iuels 35
 And so them bettar knowe to make them shun the more.

[3]

An other sort ther is that broke can not a louk
 On life ther owne, but demes hit as a yrcksome shewe,
Nor reasons lustar beare the can, reflections hers the shun,
 But ther mynd filld all with eache mans iuel al shaking
 dreads.
What dwels within abrod hit goes and gasith round about, 5
 And others sins do vew, bothe nurs and crame ther vice.
For as the hen oft in the house whan food is broght
 Runs to a cornar strait and ground doth skrape with claw,

That some wher in the dounge on grain at lest may
    find,
So fareth hit with curius mans vice, who passing ouer   10
    Institutes, lessons and skanted matter in retorik give,
And other caus suche as no man grives is axed,
    In hepes the throw the housis secret iuels and hid.
Righ wel applied is that the Egyptian said to him that axed
    What hid was that he had. That made hit hid, quoth he.   15
Nor is hit the fasyon to enter others house with out he afore
    knoke;
    Though now the portars add to for harmerling, and rings
    did hange
Vntouchet with out, served for the eare from him that enter
    wold,
    Lest stranger migh the huswife in her house surprise
Beting of her maid or chastening her man,   20
    Or shirles might heare that maiden gaue for skourge.
The prying man to all this wyl slily make his one,
    Suche one as hedes not to behold a chast and wel ruuld
    hous,
    No thogh a man in treating sort wold cal him to that sight;
    But suche as kay requires, a clog or sparred dore   25
Vncouver list, and to the vulgar sort abrode hit migt.
    Of all the wyndz the greue us most and troble bride,
Ariston telz, whos turne back strawes vs anoy,
        But curius man no neghbors cloak nor clothes estimes,
    But wales he brekes and opens dores, euen to sily maidz,   30
In sort euen suche as wind that perceth in and enters rome
    Wher Bacchus feasts, roundz and daunce he may behold,
Euen suche as in the night to Dianes temple dedicate were,
    With hedy yea espies what faultz he may find ther.

[4]

Besides, as Cleon sais, whom comedie old reproved,
    His mynd in Clopis was, his handz in Etole hid.
So mynd of curius man at onis in riche mans hous doth make
    abode

And in self time the cotage poor doth haunt and court of
   king.
And at a wedding latly made to prie the businis of eache man,   5
   Bothe of the gestz that biddid be and of the chifest all.
And so as not of peril he ventur makes therof,
   But like to him that henban tast with curius fault,
That gridy is to knowe afor he fele is reued of his like:
   So who serche the mightiars ylz first dy or understand,   10
For who disdains to looke on sun beames large and windo
   And nides wil star on bodies sun hit selfe to bold that striue
The light from him to turne, are blinded starke for here.
   Rightly said Φilippides the poete to Lisimachus who axed:
   What of myne shal I imparte as of my gift to the?   15
   What so thou wylt, quoth he, so secret none thou giue me.
For what so kingdome hathe of pleasur and ioy
   Outward set furthe be: banquetz, riches, solemne liberal
      shewes;
But if hid aught ther be, nor hit assist ne ons hit touche.
   Nor coverd be a kingly ioy whan prosperous hap arrives,   20
Nor scorne made at his sportz nor whom with bringeth
      kindly gifts.
What hidden is fearful, woful, sower and vnknowen,
   The tresor of an ouerflowing wasting ire,
Or rather habit deape in mynd to rolle revenge,
   Or zelosie of wife or sons suspect or dout of frind.   25
Fly thou this darke and thikky mysty folded cloude;
   A flasche and thoundar shal burst out whan hidden shewes.

[5]

What way therfor for fligt or shuning of the same?
   If strait thou do as said is yore to spare thy busy care,
But best if mynd thou turne helpz and delites.
O busy man, cherche what the heauen, erthe, air and sea
      afourdz.
   Wither doth delite the most, the small or great to knowe?   5
If great, than care whens son arise and wher she doth couche,
   Aske why the mone at times as man so changeth she,
Whence so great light she tooke and whens she lost repairs.

Whan left she hathe us semed how may hit be
That strait her new face faire to vs aperes   10
Slily to the circles ful increasing makes
Again whan beauty hers hathe shone unto the top
Than waning eldar growes til none be shewn.
For thes thingz be naturs secret inward workes,
   Nor doth disdaine suche science to the lerned folke.   15
But great thinges thou despice and dost not reke serche?
   Be curius than for things of les regarde.
Aske thou than of that wiche erthe brings furthe,
   Why some do florisshe stil and grine remaine,
In euery season grine the be as she that bosts herself,   20
   Some other sort in some what like to thes the shew,
Some other kind be bared left and lea, like husbandman
   That thrift neglects at ons that al his goodz hathe spent;
   For nether iust, honist nor pleasing wer suche shewe.
Than why do divers grondz brede fruts of sondry sortz,   25
   Both long, cornard, halfe round and rounded all?
Perchance of this thou carest not muche, for yl non is.
   If nides thou sekest in ivels a curius care,
Iven serpent like that fed and nourist is in poisund wood,
   Let us suche curius man bringe to stories read,   30
And gather ther suche stuf as doth include and tel.
   A plenty great of al mishaps, aboundance of all ivel,
For ther do ly the ruine of men, the wast of goodz,
   The wifes dishonor, the sarvantz baitz, the frindz slander,
The venom prepared, enuies, zelosies, wrak of frindz,   35
   The treasons huge of kings from kingdoms thrown.
Fil thou with these thy curius nice desiars:
   Pleasure taken this that bride can no wo,
Nor dolor to such folke as thou dost dwell with alle.

[6]

But as hit semes the curius man cared not for old pane.
Not suche as wonted were but sly and unfond harme he
    vews,
   That willingly may tragidies new made behold;
He recks not for to felowe comiche cause nor mery matter.

Than if he mit with one that talk of mariage makes,   5
Or sacrifice telz, or brides retourne, hideles and lasy
    The curius man hit heares, and tels how oft that he hard,
And wilz the tellar be brief in short or pas hit ouer;
    But if a sittar by do tel a tale of a dishonested maid,
Or wife that wedlok brake or cartel sent, or brothers debat,   10
    Heare he slipith not nor siuseth makes for laisur,
But sekes for more mens tongz and listen makes his eares.
    How rightly said is this: that easilar il than good to mortal
        men arrives.
And rightly said is this of curius natured man,
    For as the boxing glas the worst from flesche do draw,   15
So eares of noysy folkes the wor . . . he draweth out.
And bettar for to say, as cities haue some gates
    Vnlucky and void of noys of multitude the great,
By wiche condemned men to dy are oft conveied,
    And throw wiche the throw that filthy is and fowl,   20
And naugh by them ther goes that pure or holy is;
    So by the eares of curius men naugh good or faire doth pas,
But slaughtar talk in to ther eares has passage sure,
    And ther abides wiche wicked cursed tales them brings.
        Euer chanting teares within my house do dwell.   25
This is the muse for curius man and siren his alone,
    Nor aught than this may joy them best or please,
For curius folke have gridy wyl to heare that secret is and
        hid.
No such opens, yea to aught, if good the haue at al,
And some while the do faine suche good as ther is none.   30
    And so the nisy man that gridy is to know the ivel
Is subiect to disiase that joyes at others harmes,
    The bretherne true of spite and enuious folkes.
For enuy sorow is for good that others joys,
    A gladsomnis of ivel, the joy conciued of others wicked
        actz;
        35
And both procides of malice humor, beastlike and mad.

[7]

But yrksome so vnto eache man the opening is of his ivels

That many chuse to dy befor his secret disease the doctor
   prove.
  What if Heroφilus, Erasistratus or Esculapius, choys men
   therfor,
Carying the cures instrumentz, if standing without dores
  Wher axed wiche fistula in the thigh suche man hathe had,   5
Or wither a wife a cancer hathe in secret hiden place?
  Albeit the heltheful care be nidful of suche art,
Yet no man, I belive, but cast of wold suche on as hit wold
   axe,
  Whom no unlouked for nid uncald wold sike out others
   harme.
The busy man sikes out al thes and many wors,   10
  That with no mynd to cure, but clattar out the same.
Wherfor no nikurne the shal giue that names the cuyrous
   folk.
  For serchers we disdain and hardly brooke we can,
Not when the find that openly is brought to vew of all
  But suche as hiden be in vesselz and in packz;   15
And yet the law hit bids, and for neglect shuld smart.
  In other sort the nice men lose ther owne for others serche,
Nor dwell the chuse in country soile, for quiet fildz no care.
  But yet if after longed time the to the contry goe,
The rather vewe ther neighbors fild and pas ther owne;   20
  And axis how many oxen he hathe loste in numbar all,
And how much sowered wine he cast away with los;
  And furnist this, he quikly to the citie retournes.
But he that is a plowman right receue ful slowly wyl such
   newes
  As of fre wyl is from the citie spred abrod,   25
  And sais: than wyl fal out my diggar shal tel me tales
  On what barganes strifes haue ther ende in plea,
For even now curius of suche matter this wicked wreche
   doth walke.

[8]

But busy man the cloiny life doth hate as empty cold,
That nurs no tragicke part woful nor wicked cause,

But go the wyl to jugis seates, to markets and to portz,
  Vsing this vois: have you no newes today, wer ye in fair?
    What than? Do you belive the cities reuolt in thre hours
      time?   5
And if such tale he hathe, from his horse he lights,
  Taking hands, imbrasis the man and listing sits him by.
If met he do a man that tel can naugh: what sais thou?
  Wert thou in pleading place? Didst thou not pas the hal?
Nor hast not faln in passangers suche as last from Italye
  come?   10
  Praised be therfor the Locrens law, who did forbid
A question ons at his ret . . . . . any newes
And promist was . . . .
For as to coukes ful welcome is the numbar great of shipe,
  To fisshar eke spaum ful thik of fische find,   15
So curius men wische plenty of ivel, and businis make
  New and strange euent, wiche euer the hunt and kil.
Yea, hidely do the Thurian lawes, that charge no citizen
  think
  In comedie be vsed but to the whoring or curius men.
For adultry desiar of other pleasur, inquiry and serch also   20
  Of matter such as hid is hardly to be knowen;
For curiositie is a palssy and consumption eke that shews
  what shuld couet,
  Wiche makes the chatting vice to folow care of knowing
  muche.

[9]

And so can not be shuned, but slandar felowes the busy care,
  Wiche made Pithagoras teche fiue yeres silence to young
  men,
Wiche cal he did 'Εχεμνθια, the suafes thing that silence doth
  expres.
  Yea, hit can not be but wicked tong doth curiositie fere
For what the gladly heare the willingly readely tel,   5
  And what with hide from some the yet to others tel delite.
Wherfor this disease besides more iuels brings this to bote,

That let it doth to haue that most the seke to get;
For al men hides them wel and hides them from suche felo-
   ship,
  Nor wyl do aught or say in curius sight or eare   10
But councel defers and businis care for other time appointz,
  Vntil suche man away him get from companie thers.
And if perchance a busy man come in wher secret tale
  Or earnist aught be don, no nother wise than as the cat
In running hides his meat so sknatchz from hand that ready
   was;   15
  So that oft that other here or se may to suche,
Nor vewe nor eare may serue ther turnes,
  In fine, a curius man lacks al confidence or trust,
For rather to slaues and strangers charge our lettars we
   commit
Or trust . . . . . ler than to curius knowen frindes.   20
But Belleroϕon not lettars born against himself did open,
  But hand refrained from kingly writ with tempar suche
As he wold do with continenci from his wife.
  To be a curius man lacks tempar nowhit less
Than if adulteres part he plaid as faut no les.   25
  To this distempar this is worst that foli madnis hathe.
For in neglect of most and commen womens haunt,
  To the shut and glorious one, perhaps to the deformed,
Be caried to: what madnis more or brain siknis may be?
  So fareth hit with curius folk, who, passing by the fairest
   shews,   30
Lectors studies and disputes, others lettars breakith up,
  With eares close to neghbors wales, and whisperars adz
Wher seruaunts and women bide, yet not void of ding,
  But sure euer of slandars mark and infamy.

[10]

Yea, nideful for suche curius ons to shake of ther disease
  Remembar what ther gaines haue bene or what ther los.
For if, as Simonides said, whan sometime he opened had his
   deskes,

One fild with rewardz ful he found but empty that of
   thankes;
So if man sometime shal serche and open with curius mans
   bages,   5
Ful of unnideful, vaine and stufd with al vnpleasing thingz,
Perchance the first sight wyl him offend whan by al menes
   He shal make plain how undeliteful, vaine and skornful al
   the be.
Now go on, if entring in to ancient boukes and takes out
   The worst from them, and bouke he haue so invented,   10
As out of Homeres vers that hedles named be,
   Or out of tragical solosismz, or out of suche vers
As Archilochus againe women lewdely and ful sawsy made,
   In maner suche him selfe betraing and deciuing;
Such citi as that was wiche Φilip of wikedz wretched men
   First bilt, named therfor Πονεροπολις, as fild ful of yl.   20
Curius men, therfor, while round about the gather and
   hepe,
   Not fault of vers or poesy but crimes of other life,
Ther faultz and incongruety and about them each
   A most unpleasing ungraceful tables of other iuels,
Wiche ther owne memory fittest instrument maks.   25
   For as at Rome some pictures, and yea in dide
Formes bold of boyes, of women, the dispise, about the go
   And bide in market place wher monstars sold be,
Vewing and axing for foteles men that armes haue lik cat,
   Or thre yead men, or suche whos nek is like to camel torne,   30
Or if ther any be of kind that mixture hathe of like
   Or yuel shapd untimely birth; but if dayly the be broght
To suche a sight, short wil ther liking be, and some wyl hit
   abhor.
   So suche as curius be of others liues and liuing birth,
About the rabel and sins that haue befalne in others hous,   35
   Suche as afore the pried on, comes to ther mynd,

[lines 15 and 15a between line 14 and line 16]
Worthy do you not think him of tragical curs and ban?   15
   Ivel may the betide, the sercher out of humain woes!
Yea, hit shal not nide tragical curs, for of hit self
   Vnsemely and fruteles sleing the stooring of others sin;

Remembar the do how of the hede of others yuels
   The gather haue no credit nor profit any.

[1 1]

Hit muche may therfor avail suche maladie to driue,
   If first from dede may hap alof with vse our self inure,
And so may lerne in this motion to tempar giue our self;
   For disease increase hathe growen by customs use,
Wiche els wold turne to wors, if hit had further gone.   5
   But how hit may be don of custome let vs speke.
   Beginningz first be made of easy things sone don
And suche as comen haps and vulgar peple vse.
   For what mad matter passing by monumentz old
To neglect to read verse or writ that graffin be,   10
   Or what hard thing wer hit to pas by suche skrapings
As walz in writing receue, and not read?
   In silence warning vs that nothing ther is writen
That profit or delite may bride vs or to giue vs,
   But doth remember a writing good, be best frind of ours,   15
Or other like to this, ful vain and fild with toys,
   Wiche in them selves semes not to hurt in reading,
But slily the annoy for briding care to knowe vnnideles
     thing;
   And as the huntars rates ther houndz that usith change,
And with ther lyans them pluk back and with drawe,   20
   And kipes ther sente bothe pure and hole in right chase,
That egerlar the firm ther pace and folowe firme,
   And winding with ther sent the steps of ther game.
So aught hit fare with curius man that runs to euery gase
   In striuing for to see or lift his eare al to hire.   25
Bak kipe him and withdrawe, him selfe reserue for profit
     more.
   For as the lions walke with couver clawes and eglis eke
     ther talon,
Lest sharpnis thers and fiersnes to muche the dul,
   So mynding how al curius care haue sharpist sight
And narowly lookes on knowlege of sondry sortz,   30
   Let us not hit consume nor blunt in worsar thing.

[1 2]

In secund place, let us invre if by an others hous we go
   Not to louk in nor rolle our yees to that wiche is within
In vsing curius serche in stede of other handz,
   But ready haue Zenocrates saw, that did deny
That differens any wer wither fite or hand the house did
      enter;   5
   For guest it is a shame an inner ivel to vewe.
For thes be suche in hous most: potz that lie on ground
   Or maidens sitting stil, but nothing worth or graue.
Yet a shame hit is with glanche on suche to bend our yees,
   And hither turne our witz sharpnis and pliing mynd,   10
For to suche thinges a custom make is wicked.
   Diogines ons whan saw he did Dioχsipon in Olimpia race
In charet caried, not hable to with drawe his yea from
      woman fair,
   But bak wrying and turning nek in casting on her looke,
Behold, quoth he, a wrestlar stout with wry nek by maid is
      won.   15
   The busy men you may behold to eche shew ther hed the
      turn about,
Whan custom and care hathe made them ready to vewe eche
      thing.
But I suppos that no man ought permit his sence abrode to
      range
   Like maiden that no bringing vp hathe had such as wer
      meet.
But whan from myndz care sence is sent to businis wark,   20
   Attend suche thingz and quicly tel thy message answer,
And than againe in thy selfe with reasone make abodd
   And ther abide, not strayinge out of office charg.
But now hapz that wiche Soφocles wont is tel:
      And so as freed hors the bit   25
         That careles hand of holdar
            Did neglect.
So sence (as we have told) void of a guide or vse,
   Furthe the go and often drawe the mynd to that and more,
At length hurles him down to breke his nek.   30

Wiche makes that falsly said and brakd is of Democratus
That of purpos he pluckt out his yees, holding them to fired
    glas,
  And from the same reflection tooke, lest that the shuld
His mynd kepe shut and oft cal back to outward caus,
  Not suffering that the shud him let, left them at home,   35
That he migh bode in vnderstandings good, as shutting
    she[we]
  From windowes that to hie ways bend ther light.
But most tru hit is that rarely the do file what do the shuld,
  That vexeth oft ther mynd with busy careful thoght.
Yea, musis dipe the fur from towne did place,   40
  And night as firmest frind to knowledge great
The titeld with Euph*ρ*onen name, supposing suche vse
  And ease, whom no other care did let or hindar,
Shuld have great helpe to such things as seke the did.

[13]

  Yea, and that is not hard nor cumber hathe therin
As oft men ban the or cursing wordes aforde,
  Nor eare giue therto, but as a defe man hard them;
Or whan great pres is in the place to sit the stil,
  And if thou cans not rule the so, arise and go thi way.   5
For if thou felowe curius folke no good therof thou getz;
  But profit great shal the bifal if curius part thou shun
With violence great, thou vse and vse hit may reason lore.
  And profit taking from this grounwork and earnestar
    custom,
Right wel shalt do if theatur thou pas wher pleasant augh is
    plaid,   10
  And if thy frindz do the intreat to comedie or game, deny.
Or if comen shutz about the ringe, witsafe not.
  For as Socrates did wel warne us to take hede and beware
Of suche meat as did prouoke the unhungrie man,
  Alike he said of draughtz suche without thrust to take.   15
So we must shun suche shewes and tales as intise and allure
  Whan nide of them we haue not at all, but ar to muche.
Yea, Cirus wold not Panthea behold or vewe,

And whan Araspus told him how she worthy was to be
    seen,
That is the cause, quoth he, why more I wold refrain her.   20
    Yea, if I shuld thy counsel folowe and go to her,
Perhaps she wold perswade me againe to retourne againe,
    Euen whan my laisur aught not be to sit by her and louke
In leauing of more serius hideful matters.
    In maner suche nor Alexander wold Darius wife behold   25
Whan fame she had of beauty great and praised her muche,
    But meting mother hers, a woman old, the maiden fair
    denied.
We while ful slily looke in chamber of the wife,
    Thogh pentische like the windowe built, we think no
    harm;
The curius care our owne we suffar slip, to curius al.   30

[14]

    Hit profits also sometime that iustice may be don to pas
    ouer suche ded,
That thou mast more accustume the to flie from that as
    wrong,
    And that thou mast the bettar invre in continent sort,
Sometime forbeare the lawful companie of thi owne wif,
    Lest another time thou be inticed to other mens.   5
Briding this custom in curiositie, prove sometime that the
    doth touche, neglect;
    Nor suffer ons thy eare to give therto a hede,
And if a man wold tel the aught don at thy home, diffar him,
    And from thy eares fur set what wordz of the be said.
Edipus busy serche did wrap him in most harmes.   10
    For whan of himself he axed, as he no Corinte wez
But guest, he met with Laius, who after kild he had,
    And mother his own in mariage tok, with whom he got
    kingdom
With dowary hers; whan than happy he thoght he was,
    Againe he questioned who he was, wiche whan his w[ife]
    wold let,   15

More earnest he, the old man as guilty he wer rebukd,
Omitting no good menes to make bewrayd al that was hid.
  Than whan suspect herof his mynd had moche distract,
And old man had skrigd out, O worthi me whom nide to
    spike constrains;
  Yeat kindeled and vexed with curiositis stinge made
    answer: 20
        Compeld to heare, yeat heare I must.
So swet a sowre hit is, nor may be withstode, curiosities
    motion,
  As wound that bloudies hit self while hit is launged.
But who is freed from this disease and is of mildy spirit
  Nor gilty is of any iuel shal thus begin to say: 25
    O goddis, how wise art thou, that dost forget the yl.

[1 5]

Wherfor against al this a custoum must be made
  That strait a lettar broght may not be broken vp,
As many do, wiche whan the think ther handz to slow the
    ad to ther tithe.
  Whenseuer post do come, mete him not, nor let us change
    our pla[ce].
If so hit hap a frind ariue and say that some what he wyl
    tel him;   5
  Yea, rather if aught thou brings of profit and help.
Whan ons in Rome dispute I made, a cloin, that Domitian
    after kild,
  Who envied much the princis glory, listening to my lectur
And in the while a soldiar comming, Ceasars pistel gaue him,
  A silence made, whom none wold let to reade the sent,   10
Refuse hit nor wold hit open til endid was my reading,
  And that I had dismist my hearars and scolars;
Wherin eache man did admire the grauitie of this man.
  But whan by all menes and ways he nurris shal
Curiosities maladie and so shal make hit stronge and violent, 15
  Than easy is not hit refrain and rule,
For that by vse hit throwen is, born to things vnlawful.

Yea, the letttars teare vp and frindz secretz discover,
And sacred things behold whom no mans vewe aught se,
   And steps setz in place unfit, and kingly wordz and dedes
   do serche.   20

[16]

And tirans to, who ought al knowe, ar made most odius
   By thos men who eares thers and flatterars be called.
Therfor youngar Darius the first some hirars he had,
   αυτοκoustas cald,
   Himself mistrusting, douting others moe and fearing;
But Dionisians fuisted amonge the Siracutions suche flering
   folk   5
   Whom in changest state, whan Siracusians found, dis-
   troied.
For flatterars are of kind and stoke of curius line.
   And senthars two inquire what ivel another ment or did.
Yea, busy men iven wretched haps of neighbors thers do
   serche,
   Euen suche as fals vnto ther share though fur vnloukt for
   wer,   10
And to the vulgar folke hit tel abrode, suche newes the
   [seke].
   And said hit is that wrongged folkes beare suche name of
   curius vice;
For (as like hit was that famine had Athenes plaged, nor
   ownars wold ther corn vttar,
   But in night and secret sort grind the did ther store)
Thes walking about did note and marke ther milles noys,   15
   To wiche ther names were giuen *alitern*, propar for suche.
Of like cause, the say, were sicoϕantz cald and so surnamed,
   For whan by law hit was forbid that no man shuld figues
   gather,
Suche as them found and broght to light bar sicoϕantz name.
   Yea, that wer not unfit for curius folke to shame them ther,   20
If the knowe them gilty of suche and like andevor as the
   hold,
   Wiche hated most and griuous ar to al the haunt.

TEXTUAL AND
EXPLANATORY NOTES

ORIGINAL POEMS

Written with a Diamond

Text from John Foxe's *Acts and Monuments*, London, 1563, p. 1714;
also found in the third volume of Raphael Holinshed's *Chronicles*,
London, 1587, p. 1158. The poem must have been written around
1554–55.
1 *by* is used in its older sense of *concerning*.

Written on a Wall

This poem must also have been written c. 1554–55. The original text
is given in Paul Hentzner's *Itinerarium*, Nuremberg, 1612, p. 144.
Hentzner copied down the poem when he visited Woodstock in 1597,
but his printer could make little of the English; and Hentzner's Latin
version, given for the benefit of his Continental readers, is too free to
be of much help in restoring the original. The poem was seen, but not
copied down, by a Dutch visitor, Leo van Aitzema, in 1636, shortly
before the building was torn down. In 1757 Horace Walpole had an
English translation of Hentzner's work by Richard Bentley the
younger printed at Strawberry Hill. Bentley resorted to rewriting
the text whenever he could not understand it. For instance, his rendering of line 4 is "Hath borne me and the joys I quit." Hentzner's
mangled version is as follows:

> Oh fortune thy wresting wavering state
> Hath franght with cares my troubled witt,
> Whese witnes this present prisonn late
> Could beare mhere once was ioy sloune quitt.
> Thon causedst the gniltle to be losed
> From bandes where innocents wehre indosed,
> And consed the gniltles to be reserned,
> And freed these that death had well deserned.
> Butt allhereni canbe nothing wronghle,
> So God send to my foes althey have tonghle.

5–10 Compare these lines with Boethius I.v.30–38.

Written in Her French Psalter

These lines, along with the Queen's signature, were written on the
final page of an undated French psalter. This book, from the collection
of Her Majesty Queen Elizabeth II, was exhibited at the Stratford-

upon-Avon Poetry Festival in 1958. I have taken the text from the
Poetry Book Society Bulletin, November 1958.

2 *kind* is used in its older sense of *nature.*

The Doubt of Future Foes

This poem exists in six manuscripts and two early printed books.
The present text is based on that found in Bodleian MS. Rawlinson
poetical 108, fo. 44v, compiled, according to the *Summary Catalogue,*
about 1570. Since the poem evidently refers to the conspiracies of
Mary of Scotland, who in 1568 sought refuge in England from her
enraged subjects, this manuscript offers a very early text. Two other
sources, both printed books, give early versions, perhaps equally early.
George Puttenham used the poem as an example of rhetoric in his
Art of English Poesy, published in 1589 but largely written about
twenty years earlier (p. 207). He does not say how he got it. Henry
Harington's *Nugae Antiquae* (London, 1769) is very late in date, but
the poem there (I.58) is preceded by a letter, probably by Sir John
Harington, explaining that Lady Willoughby copied it "covertly"
from the Queen's tablet. On this letter and the sources of *Nugae
Antiquae* see Ruth Hughey, *The Arundel Harington Manuscript*
(Columbus, 1960), I, 16–26 and II, 386–388.

Puttenham and Harington have markedly different readings in a
number of places. Rawlinson poetical 108 is a better text than either
of them, but it has at least one reading which is certainly incorrect.
The rest of the manuscripts seem to have no independent authority.
British Museum Harleian 6933 (p. 22) and 7392 (p. 32) and Bodleian
Digby 138 (fo. 159) have the Puttenham text with minor variations.
The two Harington versions (*Nugae Antiquae* and Arundel, of which
British Museum Add. 28635 is a late copy) are in general but not
identical agreement. Rawlinson has a combination of readings apparently unique.

1 doubt] dread *N.A., Arundel*
4 should] would *Putt.*
   weaved] wove *N.A., Arundel*
5 joys] toys *Putt., Harl.* 7392, 6933
6 rain] rage *Rawl., Arundel*
   repent] report *N.A., Arundel*
7 supposed] suppose *N.A., Arundel*
   root upreared shall be] root of rue shall be *N.A., Arundel;* root
      of ruth shall be *Harl.* 7392; root of ruth will be *Putt.*
8 all their] of their *N.A., Arundel;* all the *Harl.* 7392, 6933
   ye] you *Harl.* 7392, 6933, *Arundel;* all *N.A.*
9 which great ambition blinds] and great ambition blind *N.A.;* with
      great ambition blind *Arundel*

10 by worthy wights] of worthy wits *Harl.* 7392
11 discord aye doth sow] eke discord doth sow *Putt.*; discord aye
   day sow *Rawl.*
12 still peace hath taught to know] still peace hath taught to flow
   N.A.; hath taught still peace to grow *Putt.*
14 not seditious sects] no seditious sects *N.A., Arundel;* it brooks no
   stranger's force *Putt.*
15 My] Our *Putt., Digby, Harl.* 7392, 6933
   sword] swords *Digby*
   through] with *Putt.*
16 their] the *N.A., Arundel*
   future joy] further joy *Arundel;* such like joy *N.A.;* lawless joy
   Harl. 6933; joy *Putt.*

On Fortune

Quoted by George Puttenham in his *Art of English Poesy*, London,
1589, p. 197, with the following introductory words: "That which
our soveraigne Lady wrate in defiance of fortune."

On Monsieur's Departure

This poem exists in three manuscripts. My text is from Bodleian
Tanner 76, p. 162, written around 1600. That in Bodleian Ashmole
781, p. 142 (c. 1620–30), is now mostly illegible, but the text of this
poem in John Nichols' *Progresses of Queen Elizabeth* (London, 1823),
II, 346, which was taken from it, shows very few variants. The third
manuscript is British Museum Stowe 962, fo. 231v (seventeenth century) where the differences are more significant. Both Ashmole and
Stowe say that Elizabeth wrote the poem on Monsieur's departure,
which would connect it with the ending of the negotiations with
Anjou in 1582. But Tanner 76, which also attributes the poem to
Elizabeth, though without any descriptive heading, places it among
poems and other papers connected with the Earl of Essex. For a dis-
cussion of the problem of authorship see Introduction, p. xiii.
Headings: *Tanner*, Sonetto; *Stowe*, E.R. upon Mounsiers depture;
   Ashmole, none.
4 but] yet *Nichols*
5 not] am not *Stowe*
6 I freeze] freeze *Stowe*
   another] my other *Nichols*
10 His] This *Stowe*
12 things] living *Stowe*
13 gentler] greater *Stowe*
   passion] passions *Stowe, Nichols*
15 so be] seek *Stowe*

17 more] *Stowe* omits
Subscriptions: *Tanner*, Eliz. Regina; *Ashmole*, Eliza Regina upon mounsyrs departure; *Stowe*, none.

Christ Was the Word

This poem, the most famous of all those attributed to Elizabeth, is almost certainly not hers. She is said to have made it as a reply to Roman Catholic priests who were examining her during Mary's reign, but neither Foxe nor Holinshed mentions it. I have given here what may be called the standard text, but many variations exist and are not worth recording. The first line sometimes appears as "Twas Christ the Word," or "He was the Word" or "God was the Word." In its first appearance in print it was attributed to John Donne in the second edition of his poems in 1635. Its second appearance in print was in Baker's *Chronicle* in 1643, where it was attributed to the Queen. It has recently turned up in a manuscript dated 1614 sold at Sotheby's on February 27, 1962 (lot 492), where it is attributed to Elizabeth. In a series of articles in *Notes and Queries* in the nineteenth century, neatly summarized by Sir John Neale in his *Essays in Elizabethan History* (London, 1958), pp. 102–103, we find that three other texts of this quatrain, presumably but not provably before 1600, have been found. None of them gives any indication of authorship.

It has been pointed out that the probable source of all these versions is a stanza from the *Pange lingua* of St. Thomas Aquinas.

> Verbum-caro panem verum
> Verbo carnem efficit,
> Fitque sanguis Christi merum,
> Et si sensus deficit,
> Ad firmandum cor sincerum
> Sola fides sufficit.

Four Knights of Nottinghamshire

This couplet was first printed by Arthur Collins in his *Peerage of England* under the article on Chesterfield. He says he got it from a manuscript history of the Clifton family among the manuscripts of Gervase Holles (presumably before 1675), which I have been unable to trace. This very late attribution is of little value.

Rebus on Noel's Name

This exchange of wit between Raleigh and Noel is found in John Manningham's diary for 1602 (British Museum Harleian 5353, fo. 83, printed version London, 1868, p. 109), and there seems to be no doubt about the authors. Agnes Latham, in her *Poems of Sir Walter Ralegh* (London, 1951), p. 138, gives a list of the other manuscripts in which these lines occur. Collins, in his *Peerage of England*, under Gainsborough, mistakenly attributes the first couplet to Elizabeth. Walpole, in his *Royal and Noble Authors*, followed his lead, and from Walpole some later writers have taken it. Frederick Chamberlin alone, in his *Sayings of Queen Elizabeth* (London, 1923), p. 39, gives the second couplet to her.

Reply to Raleigh

These lines, said by Thomas Fuller to be what Raleigh wrote on a window pane and what the Queen wrote under it, first appeared in his *Worthies of England* (London, 1662), p. 261. The ascription is too late to be of any value.

An English Hexameter

Fuller says (p. 126) that she composed this line in imitation of Sir Philip Sidney, the occasion being a visit to a grammar school. Again, the ascription is too late to be convincing.

A Latin Hexameter

This line, supposed to be Elizabeth's reply to four lines of Latin verse delivered by the Spanish ambassador as coming from his master, was written down in a manuscript dated 1614 which was sold at Sotheby's on February 27, 1962 (lot 492). It first appeared in print in George Ballard's *Memoirs of Several Ladies of Great Britain* (Oxford, 1752), p. 227, without any indication of source. From thence it was picked up by Walpole and later writers. Although the extempore composition of a Latin hexameter was by no means an impossible feat for a queen with a humanistic education, it seems unlikely that Philip II would send his demands in Latin verse. If the incident were genuine one would expect to find it mentioned in the contemporary histories. Speed was quick enough to pick up and print her Latin reply to the Polish ambassador's speech.

When I Was Fair and Young

This poem is found in five manuscripts. Bodleian Rawlinson poetical 85, fo. 1 (c. 1590–1600), attributes it to Elizabeth, and the heading, which has been scratched out, says that it was written when she "was suposed to be in love with mounsyre." British Museum Harleian 7392, p. 20 (c. 1600), has no heading, but the subscription is "ELY." Folger V.a.89, formerly 1.112 (c. 1590), has the subscription "E. of Oxford." The other two manuscripts both give it anonymously and in defective texts. Folger V.a.262, formerly 2073.4, omits all stanzas beyond the first and substitutes a new concluding stanza. Cambridge Dd.5.75, fo. 38v, also has a shortened text, the second stanza being omitted. Although some very competent modern scholars assign the poem to the Queen, I have classed it as doubtful because of the disagreement of the manuscripts and because of its style. I do not believe that she could have turned out such a facile piece of ironical wit. Her way of writing, as seen in her genuine poems, is more old-fashioned and heavy-handed.

Although it has one obvious error in line 13, Harleian 7392 seems to have the best text and is the basis for mine.

1   then] and *Rawl.*
    favor] beauty *Folger 262*
2   was I] I was *Rawl.*
    sought] wooed *Folger 262*
3   answered] said to *Folger 262*
5   in] with *Rawl.*
6   not] no *Rawl.*
7   still this spake] answered them *Rawl.;* still thus spake *Folger 89*
9   fair] brave *Folger 89*
10 Saying] And said *Rawl.*
    dainty dame for] fine dame since *Rawl.*
11 pluck your plumes] pull plums *Folger 89*
    as] that *Rawl.*
13 As soon as he had said] When he had spake these words *Rawl.*
    change] care *Folger 89*
    breast] heart *Harl.*
14 I could] since that I could *Rawl.*
15 Wherefore] Then did *Rawl.*

Epitaph Made by the Queen's Majesty

This poem appeared in John Soothern's *Pandora* (London, 1584), Sign. D1, with the heading given here. There are many problems connected with *Pandora*. It contains both odes and sonnets, many of which owe an unacknowledged debt to Ronsard and other French poets. The sonnets are all in one rhyme scheme: abba/cddc/eef/ggf. Towards the end of the volume four sonnets are attributed to the Countess of Oxford and one to the Queen, yet all these five have the same rhyme scheme as the others and are written in the same rather stilted style. Soothern in his other poems writes syllabic verse without any regard to English accent and uses eleven-syllable lines in imitation of the French. This poem has all these characteristics. No other document attributes it to Elizabeth. In fact, it remained entirely unnoticed until Flügel included it in his collection of her poems in Volume XIV of *Anglia* in 1892.

10-14 These lines freely translate the sestet of Desporte's second sonnet on the death of Diane in his *Epitaphes.*

Now Leave and Let Me Rest

This poem is found in three manuscripts: Cambridge Dd.5.75, on which my text is based; British Museum Harleian 7392; and the

Arundel manuscript printed by Ruth Hughey. British Museum Add. 28635, as noted before, is only a late copy of Arundel. It is given anonymously in Arundel and Cambridge Dd.5.75; in Harleian 7392 it is subscribed "Regina." I do not believe that Elizabeth wrote this poem. Since the Haringtons were closely connected with her it is not likely that the poem would remain anonymous in their collection in the Arundel manuscript if she had really been the author.

    4 be] are *Harl.*
   10 How] Her *Arundel*
   13 earthly] youthful *Harl.*
   14 rot] rotten *Harl., Arundel*
   15 that] the *Harl.*
   16 forgot] forgotten *Harl., Arundel*
   17 new] all *Harl.*
   18 lust desires] youth requires *Harl.*
   21 which delights] such desire *Harl.*
   22 folly] follow *Harl.*
   25 from] for *Harl.*
   27 life] place *Harl.*
   28 Whereto] Wherein *Arundel*
   30 Or] Nor *Harl., Arundel*
   31 youthful] wilfull *Harl.*
   32 stealing] creeping *Harl.*
   34 delighted] did pleasure *Arundel;* do pleasure *Camb.*
   35 age] years *Arundel*
   37 the] these *Harl.*
   41 worn] am warned *Harl.*
   42 Am] And *Harl.*
   43 might have been] ought to be *Harl.*
   45 proof] will *Arundel;* words *Harl.*

Reginae responsum

This poem, recently discovered by Professor James E. Phillips, is found in Paul Melissus' *Mele sive odae* (Nuremberg, 1580), p. 72, where it follows six elegiac couplets addressed by Melissus to Queen Elizabeth. Professor Phillips in his article in *Renaissance News* (Vol. XVI, No. 4) translates both of them into English and discusses the connections between Melissus, the Queen, and several members of her court. Melissus says that he consecrates himself and his work to her, that although a freeborn man he places himself in her service as her slave. Professor Phillips' translation of the reply, which I quote with his permission, reads as follows:

Your song is welcome, most welcome your gift; more welcome is the sweet image of your spirit. But what cause so great moves you, what impulse urges, that you, a freeborn man, desire to be a slave?

It is by no means our custom to keep poets within narrow confines, or to restrict their rights even in the smallest degree. Rather you would be made free, if you were a slave, your patroness loosening the bonds. But you are prince of poets, I a subject to a poet when you choose me as the theme of your lofty verse. What king would it shame to cherish such a poet, who makes us from demigods to be gods?

No other Latin poem by Queen Elizabeth has been preserved, so it is difficult to decide whether the attribution to her is a fiction on the part of Melissus or not. She certainly must have been well trained in the art of Latin verse by her tutors, but would she have taken the trouble to answer this and many other Latin poems addressed to her by humanists with her own hand? She may have done so, or she may have told one of her secretaries to write an answer in her name, or Melissus may have written it himself. It is worth noting that Professor Phillips reports that when Melissus reprinted his own poem to her in the 1586 edition of his *Schediasmata poetica* he omitted the *Reginae responsum*. Since there is no adequate evidence for answering these questions I have placed the poem among the dubious ones.

My text is taken from the Harvard copy of the *Mele sive odae*. In this copy there is evidence of a different setting of type on page 72 (F4 verso), for there are two variants, noted below, from the British Museum copy used by Professor Phillips.

2   tui.] tui *BM*
4   velis] vellis *BM*

TRANSLATIONS

The Thirteenth Psalm

This translation, or rather free paraphrase, is found at the end of *A Godly Meditation of the Soul*, London, 1548 (*STC* 17320), a translation by Elizabeth of the meditations of Margaret of Navarre. It is headed by the following statement: "The xiii Psalme of David, called *Dixit insipiens*, touched afore of my lady Elizabeth." The paraphrase must have been made from the Vulgate, since this Psalm is numbered 14 in the English Bibles. Rhyming paraphrases were usually much freer than prose versions, as can be seen by comparing the Sternhold and Hopkins rhymed translation of this Psalm with the Vulgate and the English Bibles.

11   *wode.* Modern English "furious."

Petrarch

This translation was first printed by Ruth Hughey in 1960 in her edition of the Arundel Harington manuscript. My modernized text is based on hers by permission of the publishers, the Ohio State University Press. The heading is merely "Triumphe Petrarcke," but the initials E. R. are written in the margin at the end of the poem. Beneath these initials, Miss Hughey's note tells us, is a contraction in a different hand which may be either *scr* (scripsit) or *sec* (secundus). The latter reading might refer to the second year of the Queen's reign, but this is not certain. At any rate, Miss Hughey's opinion is that the use of the hand B in the manuscript shows that the poem was copied some time early in her reign. In spite of the necessities of rhyme her translation is done in exactly the same number of lines as the original, but it uses a different rhyme scheme. The Italian is in terza rima.

24-25   The Italian has "and one made more fair." The *and* is necessary to the sense in the English.

26-35   This is a puzzling passage as translated. *Him* is Time, who in eternity stands still ("on one foot"). His three parts are past, present, and future.

42   Instead of *a toil* the Italian has *our toil.*

54   This sentence, like its Italian original, lacks a main clause. *Whose* refers to God.

87   *Stound* here means time or hour (Italian *allor*).

88 *Which* refers to the nouns in line 86.
  kind. Used in its older sense of "nature."

Seneca

This translation of the second chorus in *Hercules Oetaeus* is found in Bodleian MS. e Museo 55. It is not in the Queen's own hand. The manuscript was given to the Bodleian by Dr. Robert Clay and the heading "A translation of Q. Elizabeth ex dono D. Clay" is in his hand. This would date the inscription, though not necessarily the text, as probably in the first decade of the seventeenth century. There are a number of indications of careless copying from the original. The question of authenticity is puzzling. The English style sounds like Elizabeth's, but the method of translation is totally different from that which she used in making versions of Boethius, Horace, Plutarch, or Petrarch. The Seneca is a very free paraphrase in which it is often impossible to know whether one is reading a passage which is meant to be a translation of the Latin or an original addition. One third of the first thirty-one lines, for instance, have no parallel in the Latin. For what it is worth—and that may be little—I will point out that the same mistake of translating *Corus* as the east wind which is found in Elizabeth's Boethius (IV.v.13) occurs here at line 74. There seems to be no way of determining when this version was made, if it is hers. We know, however, that she was making translations of other Latin classics in the first decade of her reign, and perhaps this should be put among them. There is no mention of it by anyone before Park's edition of Walpole's *Royal and Noble Authors* in 1806.

Of considerable interest is the fact that these lines are fairly regular blank verse instead of the rough and uncertain iambics of varying lengths found in her other versions from Latin and Greek. If it were mainly an exercise in English versification rather than in translating Latin, then the failure to follow the text more closely would be understandable. But one must admit that "J.S." (John Studley), who published his English version of *Hercules Oetaeus* in 1581, also adds and expands freely. There does not appear to be any relation between his translation, which is in six-line stanzas, and this one.

In spite of many doubts I include this piece among Elizabeth's genuine works because of its similarity in style with her other verse writings, but it would not surprise me if evidence turned up some day to disprove her authorship. I have used Flügel's careful transcription in *Anglia*, Vol. XIV, as the basis of my text, but it has been checked with the manuscript and corrected in a few places.

5 *geason.* Scarce, uncommon.
7 *choice.* The Latin shows that the word should be *thou*. Probably a scribal error.

16 *passed*. Almost certainly a scribal error for *passage*.

26 *icy*. Slippery, uncertain.

48 *please his lack not so*. Unintelligible. The previous words in this sentence sufficiently translate *avidis, avidis natura parum est*.

50 *harbor Rome*. Rome is not mentioned in the Latin, which merely says *reges regumque lares*.

55–56 This passage can be understood better when one knows that Renaissance texts read *opes quas donet* (or *donat*) in place of the *ponat* found in modern texts. The idea, possibly confused by faulty copying, seems to be "goods which he may with pleasure give to other." The older reading destroys Seneca's meaning in this passage.

74 *eastern*. The Latin *Corus* means northwest.

97 *The*. Scribal error for *With* as the Latin (*dira lampade*) makes clear.

98 *adorns*. This cannot be what was meant. Either *adorned* or *adored* would make an intelligible rendering of *coluere*.

105 *wonted*. This word is written twice in the MS.
     worned. It is not clear what this word was meant to be. It is not clearly written in the MS.

109 *larger scope*. Modern texts read *tenuit placidas Daedalus oras*, but all the early texts I have seen have *Latias . . . oras*. *Latias* often appears without the initial capital, and the Queen seems to have misread it as *latas*.

117 *flee*. All the early texts read *volet* here instead of *sonet*.

INTRODUCTORY NOTE TO THE
PUBLIC RECORD OFFICE MANUSCRIPT
(BOETHIUS, PLUTARCH, HORACE)

The translations from Boethius, Plutarch, and Horace are found in the Public Record Office in London (Domestic Elizabeth 289). All three are preserved together, although notes on the manuscripts indicate that the Boethius was done in 1593 and the other two in 1598. These notes are given in full in Caroline Pemberton's edition in the Early English Text Society publications (Vol. 113, 1899). The two later pieces are entirely in the Queen's hand; the Boethius, however, is partly in her hand and partly in the hands of secretaries. Usually they wrote the prose and she the metres, but in Book IV a secretary wrote metre v and metre vi, 1–18 and 30–47; of metre ii we have copies by both Elizabeth and a secretary.

Notes on the manuscripts make the claim that the Boethius was done in twenty-five or thirty days' elapsed time (the notes do not agree in their computation) and that on about half of these days she was otherwise occupied and did no translating. Furthermore, it is claimed that she never put in more than one or two hours' work on the days when she did do so. Whatever one may think as to the credibility of these extraordinary statements, it is evident that the translation must have been done at great speed, and therefore with many faults. Corrections in the manuscript and the mixture of different hands show that what we have is first draft and not a revised fair copy.

The speed of Elizabeth's translation accounts for most of the errors and obscurities pointed out in Miss Pemberton's notes. She probably never stopped to use a dictionary, and in her haste she often left out lines in the Latin. At other times she evidently forgot to write down words that she must have translated in her mind, usually the verb. And she sometimes uses meanings of words which are correct, in the sense that they are found in the dictionary, but not suitable to the context she is dealing with. In general, she seems to be trying to translate literally, line for line whenever possible. This led her all too often to follow the Latin word order to the confusion of the English. She also frequently omits definite and indefinite articles and personal pronouns, and she puts possessive pronouns after the nouns instead of before them. Throughout her versions of the metres one sees an extraordinary attempt to imitate in English the conciseness of the Latin. In some of them she achieves the difficult feat of using only the same number of lines as the original.

If it were not for the fact that we have these metres written with indentations and uneven line endings in Elizabeth's own hand we might doubt whether they were intended to be in verse. The suspicion sometimes arises that they are merely line-for-line literal translations, like a student's interlinear help, but on the whole the evidence is against this, especially as a similar kind of rough iambic rhythm in the translation of Plutarch is called "English miter" in a note by a secretary at the end of it. I see no evidence that Elizabeth had anything like imitation of the classical metres in mind, and the speed with which she was working would have prevented her from trying anything as difficult as that. She was evidently merely trying to impose some sort of iambic pattern on her painfully literal rendering without worrying whether it came out even or not. When not in haste, she could write fairly good iambics, as her other poems show. She does, however, vary her line length in imitation of the Latin metres she is translating, as a brief look at the metres of Book I, especially the last metre, will show.

My text of these three translations makes use of Miss Pemberton's, but it has been checked throughout against a film of the manuscript, and I have corrected some errors and omissions. Her edition contains a Latin text of the Boethius as well as the English. This is very helpful in understanding some of the difficult passages, but Miss Pemberton was not aware that the Renaissance editions of the classics often had different readings from those of modern times. She therefore accuses the Queen of mistranslation in a number of passages where the latter actually rendered quite correctly the words she had before her. What text she used I have not been able to determine, and therefore I have not printed any Latin text in this book. Nevertheless, a comparison of the twenty sixteenth-century editions in the Harvard Library has enabled me to narrow the field very considerably. All these editions have *arma* instead of *arva* in II.v.18, *tecto* instead of *texto* in III.ii.22, *devio* instead of *devios* in III.viii.1, and *captos* instead of *captus* in IV.ii.8. In some other places they have readings which are in agreement with Bieler's recent edition (Turnholt, 1947) but not with Miss Pemberton's Latin text. Fourteen of the twenty have *angustam* instead of *augustam* in the opening sentence of III. par. 2. This reading is translated by Elizabeth, but she also follows the obvious error of *fructibus* for *fruticibus*, which is only found in three editions: Rouen, 1503; Cologne, 1504; and Leipzig, 1510. Although she might have misread one of these words for the other, it is more reasonable to suppose that she wrote *fruits* rather than *bushes* because that was what she saw. Therefore I assume that she used a copy of one of these editions or of an edition (or a manuscript) which I have not seen containing the same readings.

Since this book is an edition of Elizabeth's verse and not a study of her ability and her methods as a translator I have not imitated Miss Pemberton's very full notes on these matters. Her work, even though it neglects the Renaissance editions, will provide valuable assistance to anyone wishing to make such a study. I have only annotated those passages where I could correct or amplify hers.

Contrary to the practice in the rest of this book, the material from the Public Record Office is given in the original spelling. I have done this because most of it is in the Queen's own hand, a condition which does not exist in any of the other manuscripts used. Even those few passages from the metres of Boethius which are not in her own hand have been given *literatim* for the sake of comparison with the Queen's spelling. It will be at once observed that she had many peculiarities. She used the letter *i* for the long *e* sound (*nides* for *needs*) very often but not always, and she uses a final *z* instead of a final *s* very often but again not always. In fact, the one certain thing about her spelling is that, with the exception of a very few words like *wiche* and *hit* (for *it*), it is never absolutely consistent. She quite often writes final *ar* in place of *er* (*wondar* for *wonder*), but the modern ending is not unusual. She uses *i* and *y* as vowels quite indiscriminately and similarly *i* and *j* as consonants. She sometimes put a *t* at the end of words like *sight* and *naught* but is very likely to omit it. And she will spell a simple word like *search* in five different ways on different occasions. But when one has read her spelling for some time it is not hard to spot the point at which a secretary has replaced her, as at line 19 of Book IV, metre vi.

I have regularized according to modern practice the utterly meaningless use of capitals in the manuscript; and I have supplied modern punctuation, though some of the more difficult passages defy any attempt to do so. Finally, the reader is warned that when Elizabeth writes *the* it may mean *thee* or *they* or the definite article as the context demands.

Boethius

I.i.16   *yees*. Elizabeth usually spells *eyes* this way.

ii.17   *solne*. swollen

v.22   *dok*. Since the Latin is *Sirius* this is the *dog* star.

vi.1   *sm^e*. What this contraction stands for is difficult to guess. Miss Pemberton queries *smitten*.

vi.20   *rachelous*. Hasty. The Latin is *praecipiti*.

II.v.5   *louse*. This is a common Elizabethan spelling for *loose*. The Latin is *solvere*.

     son got. Soon (i.e. easily) gotten.

II.v.18   *weapons*. All sixteenth-century texts read *arma* instead of *arva* found in modern texts.

vi.15   *frantique*. The textual tradition represented by Elizabeth's text has *pravi* here, as do modern editions. In some early texts it is *insani*.

III.i.2   *fruit*. The farmer should, in the correct text, free his field of bushes (*fruticibus*), but Elizabeth's text read *fructibus*.

i.5   *flies*. Modern readers would prefer *bees*, but Elizabeth's word, which she uses twice for the Latin *apes*, meant in her time any winged insect (see III.vii.3).

ii.8   *gives*. This is the Elizabethan word for *chains*. In the MS the word occurs also at the end of line 7.

ii.21   *eues*. Elizabeth's text read *tecto* (roof); modern texts have *texto* (wicker cage).

v.10   *expel*. This is an example of Elizabeth's disregard of the nature of the English language. The meaning, of course, is "to expel," but she omits this expected sign of the infinitive several times in these metres.

viii.1   *begiling*. Miss Pemberton objected to this because she did not know what Elizabeth's text was. Modern texts have here *miseros tramite devios*, but sixteenth-century texts read *miseros tramite devio*.

ix.16 *glimmers.* Miss Pemberton failed to transcribe this word. It must represent the Latin *glomeravit*, for all the other words in this sentence are translated. It sounds like a careless slip, for the Queen could not possibly have supposed that *glimmers* was the English meaning of *glomeravit*.

xii.42 *feere.* Elizabethan word for companion or mate.

xii.59 *Et sic bene.* Not in Boethius, but added by the Queen as a comment. It would seem to mean "and well done," possibly indicating her approval of the punishment of lawbreakers.

IV.i.10 *sorteth.* Joins. The Latin is *coniungat*.

i.11 *soldiar.* The Latin is *miles*, but more modern translators render it as *companion*.

ii This metre is found in the MS once in a secretary's hand and once in the Queen's hand. The spelling here given is the Queen's. For what interest they may have I add the following variations in the secretary's spelling.

ii.1 Thos] Those

ii.5 thretes] threats

ii.9 ther] theyr

ii.10 Straightned] Strayghtenid

ii.12 Hire] Heere
ther] their

ii.13 sturred] styerid

ii.14 wers] wears (translates the Latin *fatigat*)

ii.15 slippar] slipper

iii.4 *feare.* Modern spelling *fair* (translates Latin *pulchra*).

iii.37 *woundz.* This translates the correct textual reading *vulnere*. Miss Pemberton's Latin text has *ulcere*, a reading almost always rejected by editors.

v This metre is not in the Queen's hand.

v.13 *southest.* The Latin says northwest (*Corus*). The same error occurs in the translation of a Senecan chorus attributed to the Queen, line 74. See p. 81.

v.20 *vulgar fleete.* If this, as seems certain, is the rendering of *mobile vulgus*, then *stupet*, the verb in this clause, has not been translated.

vi In this metre lines 1–18 and 30–48 are not in the Queen's hand.

vi.21 *by.* This word is not in the MS but is required by the meaning.

vi.48 This line has been considerably crossed out and amended in the MS. Miss Pemberton reads it as "Back to the cause them made bend."

vii.18 *peaced.* Miss Pemberton correctly conjectured that this is an old word usually spelled *pesed*, meaning "weighed down." The Latin is *gravior*.

V.ii.4   *pears*. Miss Pemberton thinks that this means *peers* or *appears*. Since the Latin is *perrumpere* I assume the meaning to be *pierce*.

   iv.3   *lest motes*. A difficult passage. Miss Pemberton reads *notes*, but the initial letter looks more like *m* to me. The phrase translates *corporibus extimis*, and I think Elizabeth in her haste, and jumping at a meaning, thought it read *exiguis*.

   iv.6   *sea*. Miss Pemberton reads *seaying*, but in the MS the last three letters seem to have been crossed out. The Latin is *aequore*.

    v.9   This line as it stands makes no sense. Elizabeth failed to translate, or at any rate to write down, the verb, *ingravare*. The downward-looking faces of the beasts weigh down their dulled senses.

Horace

The translation of Horace's *Art of Poetry* was never finished, ending at line 178 of the Latin. Not so painfully literal as the version of the Boethian metres, this translation sticks pretty closely to the text and contains no material added by the Queen. Although it shows in general a good understanding of the Latin, there are a number of mistranslations and some unintelligible lines. There are fewer deletions and corrections than in the Plutarch, but one has the suspicion that, like the Boethius, it was done in haste. Some of the errors in reading suggest not only haste but possibly failing eyesight. The Queen was sixty-five when she did this version, and she probably scorned to use eyeglasses. I have not been able to discover what text of the Latin she used, but, as the notes will reveal, a number of readings were common in the Renaissance which are no longer found in modern editions.

   14   *iniud*. This seems to represent the Latin *aequa*, but the English meaning is obscure.

   15   *lein*. The Latin equivalent is *veniam*, meaning indulgence or pardon. Elizabeth's meaning is obscure, but perhaps the word is related to the modern English *lien*, a claim on property.

   20   *pace*. Evidently *patch* is meant. The Latin is *pannus*.

   22   *crake*. This is a poor translation of the Latin *ambitus*. Elizabeth must have been thinking of the sound of running water, but even then the idea of croaking, or of creaking, does not fit very well.

   41   *stage play*. This is the wrong meaning of *ludus* in this passage. Horace was thinking of a school.

   60   *Cethes*. Latin *Cethegi*. Miss Pemberton misreads as *Lethes*.

   67   *weany*. Young, not full grown.

   75   *by northern winde*. The meaning of the Latin is that the ships

were protected *from* the northern wind, not *by* it. Elizabeth, who frequently got her winds wrong (see notes to Boethius IV.v.13 and Plutarch 1.17), first wrote *southern* and then corrected it.

77   *coustumed. Accustomed,* i.e. it had been a marsh a long time. This renders the Latin *diu* and leaves *sterilis* untranslated.

84   *fors.* Correct translation of *vis,* which many sixteenth-century texts have in place of *ius,* now regarded as correct.

87   *onjvend.* Can this be meant for *uneven,* which Elizabeth might have spelled *oniven?* The Latin is *impariter.*

102   *scene.* The Latin is *coena,* a banquet. Already thinking of the drama, the Queen apparently misread it as *scaena.*
    wordiest. Elizabethan spelling for *worthiest.*
    decerns. This word has no equivalent in the Latin and seems to make no sense.

106   *face.* The wrong meaning of the Latin *ore,* which here means *mouth.*

109   *vase.* Elizabeth has confused the two meanings of *ampullas.* Here it means not vases but inflated language.

117   *place.* An unintelligible rendering of *loqueris,* meaning speak.

122   The last word is bound in and cannot be read.

126   *army all.* The Latin has *Romani . . . equites peditesque* with a pun on the two meanings of *equites,* but the Queen missed the point and thought it meant "the whole army."

127   *Dauus or Eros.* This line puzzled the sixteenth-century editors, who render it in various ways. In modern texts (and in the best Renaissance ones) it reads *divusne . . . an heros.* Several early editions read *Davusne . . . an Eros,* but all of these that I have seen also have the reading *ius* instead of *vis* at line 72. Other early editions read *Davus* and *Heros.* Elizabeth may merely have dropped the *H,* thinking it a medieval corruption.

133   The last word in this line is illegible. Miss Pemberton reads "shipp," but the meaning is obscure.

140   *comme.* Common.

142   *vntouche.* The final *d* probably carelessly omitted in writing. The Latin is *ignota.*

146   *act.* The meaning of the Latin is to jump into a narrow place or well (*artum*), but in early texts the word is spelled *arctum.* Elizabeth either misread as *actum* or had a text with *actum* as a misprint.

159   *grandfathers shell.* A tantalizing mistranslation of *ab ovo* (from the egg), since *ovo* could mean eggshell and *avo* would be *grandfather.*

160 *best menes*. A strange mistranslation of the famous *medias res*. Miss Pemberton suggests that Elizabeth misread *medias* as *melius*.

173 *color*. Since the Latin is *iram*, this means *choler*.

Plutarch

It is impossible to guess why Elizabeth translated Plutarch's prose essay on curiosity from the *Moralia* into English verse. In fact, if it were not labeled as "miter" by her secretary and written down with indentations by her own hand one might doubt whether it was intended to be verse. There is little attempt to keep strictly to the beat, but most of the lines have a sort of iambic rhythm, and quite a number of them do come out as good iambics. Although they range in length from five to nine feet, the normal line seems to be six feet, which was perhaps the Queen's approximation of the classical hexameter in English.

There are many corrections and substitutions in the manuscript. Miss Pemberton, in her transcription for her edition in the Early English Text Society publications, does not follow any consistent method in dealing with them. Sometimes she includes a crossed-out word if she thinks it makes better sense, and sometimes she does not. Elizabeth herself does not always seem to know what she is doing, so that one gets the impression that this translation, like the Boethius, was done hurriedly. But in this case we lack any such direct statement as was made about the former. I have tried to be more consistent than Miss Pemberton, but I am not sure that I have always succeeded. There is a great temptation to produce a text that will make sense even at the expense of falsifying what the manuscript offers. Sensible punctuation, almost entirely lacking in the manuscript, is a great help to understanding the text, but Miss Pemberton often fails in this respect. I have tried, in my punctuation, to follow the sense of the Greek, but the overlong, loosely constructed sentences and the difficulty of understanding Elizabeth's curious way of expression have often defeated my best efforts. Sixteenth-century texts of the *Moralia* had no chapter divisions, and the Queen had none. I have introduced them to facilitate reference to modern editions and to Miss Pemberton's text, which has them.

As will be seen from the note to 3.30 the Queen was acquainted with some of the Latin translations of Plutarch, but there are other passages where she does not follow any of them. It seems extremely unlikely, therefore, that she made her whole translation from a Latin version. Words written with Greek letters in 9.3, 10.20 and 16.3 show that she had the Greek text before her. In view of the fact that she gives extra indentation to all of Plutarch's quotations from other authors, showing that she recognized them as quotations, one might think that it would be possible to determine what her text was, since not all the Renaissance editions of Plutarch print the quotations in this way but include them within the solid paragraph without any break. In fact, of the editions printed in Greek, only that of Basel, 1574, makes the quotations identifiable. Unfortunately for our theory, this edition prints ἀλιζόνος with a capital alpha and Ρούστικος with a capital rho, and this conflicts with the evidence discussed in my explanatory notes to 1.36 and 15.7–9. The edition printed at Basel in 1542, on the other hand, prints both of these words with small letters, which would account for Elizabeth's translation, but it does not indent the quotations. Since we have shown that Elizabeth had some acquaintance with the Latin versions, it should be pointed out that the Basel, 1573, edition of the Latin does indent the quotations and does spell Rusticus with a small *r*, but it translates ἀλιζόνος as *Doricus Isthmus,* which the Queen did not follow. The translation by Erasmus in the Stephanus edition of the *Opera* (1572) indents the quotations but spells Rusticus with a capital *R. Isthmus* appears without the qualifying adjective. One can only conclude that she had a manuscript or that she had several books before her and constructed an eclectic text of her own. However, this should have led her to reject *rusticus* and realize that a man's name was meant and not the name of a class of people.

1.17   *northern.* The Greek says *southern.* See notes to Boethius IV.v.13 and Horace 75.

1.25   *that.* This word is in the MS but crossed out.

1.29   MS torn.

1.36   The meaning of κατ'ἀλιζόνος, here translated "to bay," is a puzzle, since the word is unknown elsewhere. It may be a place name—some editors and translators so give it—but Elizabeth was evidently using a text which spelled it with a small alpha. Other Renaissance translators guessed that it meant an island or an isthmus, since other words of similar form have to do with salt, salt water, or the sea.

2.1   Miss Pemberton inserts *that* between *tell* and *Lamia.* The word is in the MS, but crossed out. It makes better sense to omit it.

3.30   This reference to nocturnal revels in the temple of Diana is not in Plutarch. It comes from the Latin paraphrase of Sagundinus or Erasmus. They add at this point *"quae noctu celebrantur Dianae,"* a phrase not found in the Latin versions of Xylander or Cruserius.

4.9   *like.* Probably a mistake for *life,* which is what the Greek means.

5.2   This and the preceding line are badly scratched out and hard to read.

5.3   Doubtless Elizabeth meant to write *to* before *helpz.*

5.16   *reke.* Care to.

5.22   *lea.* Fallow.

5.24   Not in the Greek nor the Latin paraphrases. It is one of several moral tags inserted by the Queen.

6.4   *felowe.* Have fellowship with.

6.11   *siuseth.* Probably a mistake for *scuses.*

6.16   MS torn.

6.31   *nisy.* Curious. See 5.37.

7.8   *man.* This word is required by the Greek, but in the MS it is impossible to tell what word was meant. Miss Pemberton transcribes it as ma[n]ar.

7.12   *nikurne.* Miss Pemberton prints *inknowne* but adds that the word "looks more like *nikurne.*" It certainly does, but I can attach no meaning to either collection of letters. The Greek gives no help here, for the Queen is paraphrasing too freely at this point to permit identification of individual words.

8.1   *cloiny.* Clowny, i.e. countrified.

8.12–13 MS torn.

8.18   *think.* Obviously a mistake for *thing.*

8.19   *whoring.* The first three letters are illegible. Miss Pemberton reads *murdering,* but the Greek word means adulterers.

9.3   *suafes.* Miss Pemberton suggests *suavest,* and this very passage is cited in the *Oxford English Dictionary* under the meaning "pleasant, agreeable."

9.4   *fere.* Used here as a verb meaning to accompany.

9.15   *sknatchz.* Perhaps *sknatching* in MS.

9.20   MS torn.

9.33   *ding.* The Greek word means *danger,* which is perhaps what the Queen meant to write. The *Oxford English Dictionary* gives "violent push or commotion" as a nineteenth-century dialect meaning for *ding.*

10.18 *sleing the stooring.* This is unintelligible as it stands. Since the Greek refers to a collection of other people's sins, the Queen probably meant to write "being the storing." Miss Pemberton reads *sleing,* but the first letter has been written over so as to be illegible.

10.30 *camel torne.* Probably the final d was omitted from *torne,* and the meaning is "with neck turned (i.e. curved) like a camel." The Greek word means ostrich-headed or sparrow-headed.

11.10 *neglect.* Over this word is written *disdain,* but neither is crossed out.

12.11 *wicked.* Over this word is written *yl,* but neither is crossed out.

12.40 *musis dipe.* Miss Pemberton says, correctly, that there is no equivalent for *dipe* in the Greek. However, I think Elizabeth is translating τα μουσεῖα as "the Muses deep" (i.e. profound, learned), although the word literally means temples of the Muses.

13.12   This line is rather puzzling. The Greek means "when shouts are heard on the race-course or in the circus, turn not around." I take it that *if comen shutz* means "if the common people shouts." *Witsafe* is an old form of *vouchsafe*.

14.11   *wez*. Was.

14.15   MS torn.

14.19   *O worthi me*. Probably meant for *Woe worth me*, a common Elizabethan expression of dismay.

15.7–9   Elizabeth confused this passage by supposing that Rusticus, a proper name here, meant simply a rustic (clown), by leaving it unclear who killed whom (actually Domitian killed Rusticus), and by supposing that the clown envied Domitian, whereas it was Domitian who envied Rusticus. Some sixteenth-century editions spelled Rusticus with a small *r*, which might have started the confusion, but on this point see p. 89.

15.9   *pistel*. Epistle.

15.10   *the sent*. The thing sent, the letter. The Greek is ἐπιστολήν.

16.3   *youngar*. Modern texts of the Greek have νόθος, but Renaissance texts read νέος. Elizabeth correctly translated the text she had.

      αutoκoustas. The correct spelling is ὠτακουστάς.

16.5   *fuisted*. Miss Pemberton reads *mixed*, but the MS is quite clear. "Foisted" is a good translation of the Greek.

16.6   *changest*. This must be a mistake for *changed*.

16.8   *senthars*. Meaningless as it stands. Miss Pemberton suggests *censors*. The Greek word means informers.

      two. Probably a mistake for *too*, since no number is mentioned in the Greek.

16.11   *seke*. Illegible in the MS. Miss Pemberton's conjecture, which I have used, seems reasonable.